Civil Liberties and War

Other books in the Issues on Trial series:

| Civil Liberties and War

Jamuna Carroll, Book Editor

GREENHAVEN PRESS

An imprint of Thomson Gale, a part of The Thomson Corporation

Detroit • New York • San Francisco • San Diego • New Haven, Conn.
Waterville, Maine • London • Munich

LIBRARY OF CONGRESS CATALOGING-IN-PUBLICATION DATA

Civil liberties and war / Jamuna Carroll, book editor.
  p. cm. -- (Issues on Trial)
  Includes bibliographical references and index.
  ISBN 0-7377-2503-6 (lib. : alk. paper)
1. War and emergency powers--United States--Cases. 2. Civil Rights--United States--Cases.
I. Carroll, Jamuna. II. Series.
  KF5900.A7C58 2006

  342.73'0412--dc22

                                        2005052761

Printed in the United States of America
10 9 8 7 6 5 4 3 2 1

Contents

The Supreme Court determined in *New York Times Co. v. United States* (1971) that newspapers cannot be prevented from publishing the Pentagon Papers, a top-secret history of U.S. involvement in the Vietnam War.

Chapter 4: According Due Process Rights to Enemy Combatants

A Supreme Court justice dissenting in *Hamdi* claims that in wartime, the government's powers trump citizens' rights.

Foreword

The U.S. courts have long served as a battleground for the most highly charged and contentious issues of the time. Divisive matters are often brought into the legal system by activists who feel strongly for their cause and demand an official resolution. Indeed, subjects that give rise to intense emotions or involve closely held religious or moral beliefs lay at the heart of the most polemical court rulings in history. One such case was *Brown v. Board of Education* (1954), which ended racial segregation in schools. Prior to *Brown*, the courts had held that blacks could be forced to use separate facilities as long as these facilities were equal to that of whites.

For years many groups had opposed segregation based on religious, moral, and legal grounds. Educators produced heartfelt testimony that segregated schooling greatly disadvantaged black children. They noted that in comparison to whites, blacks received a substandard education in deplorable conditions. Religious leaders such as Martin Luther King Jr. preached that the harsh treatment of blacks was immoral and unjust. Many involved in civil rights law, such as Thurgood Marshall, called for equal protection of all people under the law, as their study of the Constitution had indicated that segregation was illegal and un-American. Whatever their motivation for ending the practice, and despite the threats they received from segregationists, these ardent activists remained unwavering in their cause.

Those fighting against the integration of schools were mainly white southerners who did not believe that whites and blacks should intermingle. Blacks were subordinate to whites, they maintained, and society had to resist any attempt to break down strict color lines. Some white southerners charged that segregated schooling was *not* hindering blacks' education. For example, Virginia attorney general J. Lindsay Almond asserted, "With the help and the sympathy and the love and respect of the white people of the South, the colored man has risen under that educational process to a place of eminence and respect throughout the nation. It has served him well." So when the Supreme Court ruled against the segregationists in *Brown*, the South responded with vociferous cries of protest. Even government leaders criticized the decision. The governor of Arkansas, Orval Faubus, stated that he would not "be a party to any attempt to force acceptance of change to which the people are so overwhelmingly opposed." Indeed, resistance to integration was so great that when black students arrived at the formerly all-white Central High School in Arkansas, federal troops had to be dispatched to quell a threatening mob of protesters.

Nevertheless, the *Brown* decision was enforced and the South integrated its schools. In this instance, the Court, while not settling the issue to everyone's satisfaction, functioned as an instrument of progress by forcing a major social change. Historian David Halberstam observes that the *Brown* ruling "deprived segregationist practices of their moral legitimacy.... It was therefore perhaps the single most important moment of the decade, the moment that separated the old order from the new and helped create the tumultuous era just arriving." Considered one of the most important victories for civil rights, *Brown* paved the way for challenges to racial segregation in many areas, including on public buses and in restaurants.

In examining *Brown*, it becomes apparent that the courts play an influential role—and face an arduous challenge—in shaping the debate over emotionally charged social issues. Judges must balance competing interests, keeping in mind the high stakes and intense emotions on both sides. As exemplified by *Brown*, judicial decisions often upset the status quo and initiate significant changes in society. Greenhaven Press's Issues on Trial series captures the controversy surrounding influential court rulings and explores the social ramifications of such decisions from varying perspectives. Each anthology highlights one social issue—such as the death penalty, students' rights, or wartime civil liberties. Each volume then focuses on key historical and contemporary court cases that helped mold the issue as we know it today. The books include a compendium of primary sources—court rulings, dissents, and immediate reactions to the rulings—as well as secondary sources from experts in the field, people involved in the cases, legal analysts, and other commentators opining on the implications and legacy of the chosen cases. An annotated table of contents, an in-depth introduction, and prefaces that overview each case all provide context as readers delve into the topic at hand. To help students fully probe the subject, each volume contains book and periodical bibliographies, a comprehensive index, and a list of organizations to contact. With these features, the Issues on Trial series offers a well-rounded perspective on the courts' role in framing society's thorniest, most impassioned debates.

Introduction

While managing the United States during the Civil War, President Abraham Lincoln adopted policies that curtailed the civil liberties of citizens. Amid riots and the secession of rebellious Southern slave states from the nation, Lincoln implemented measures that he hoped would secure the North's victory and guard against espionage. Among them was the suspension of the writ of habeas corpus, the constitutional right of inmates to a hearing to determine whether they should be released. This act allowed officials to detain suspected traitors and prevent them from harming the country without having to prove them guilty of a crime.

Lincoln's suspension of habeas corpus was not an isolated incident. In fact, the United States has a history of restricting the rights of Americans in time of war. On numerous occasions the government has asserted that the need to maintain order and safety trumps civil liberties. Traditionally, the Supreme Court has supported the executive branch in its wartime efforts even if that means abridging freedoms. This is because the Constitution contains exceptions to rights in times of national crisis. For example, it specifies that the privilege of habeas corpus may be revoked "when in Cases of Rebellion or Invasion the public Safety may require it."

The Civil War was such a time, according to President Lincoln. He cautioned: "Disloyal persons are not adequately restrained by the ordinary processes of law from . . . giving aid and comfort in various ways to the insurrection." To prevent having civil court judges release defendants for advocating insurgency (speech which is normally protected), Lincoln allowed these suspects to be imprisoned without trial. The Supreme Court later ruled that Congress, not the president, has the power to renege the right to habeas corpus.

Also during the Civil War, Lincoln limited rights to free

During the Civil War Abraham Lincoln suspended the constitutional right of imprisoned suspects to receive a hearing. Lincoln also limited free speech and press rights. Library of Congress

expression and a free press. The First Amendment Center contends,

> Lincoln seized the telegraph lines ... and issued an order prohibiting the printing of war news about military move-

ments without approval. People were arrested for wearing Confederate buttons.... Government officials shut down the *Chicago Times* for excessively criticizing the Lincoln administration.

President Lincoln's actions greatly alarmed citizens who felt that even in time of war, due process and speech rights should be preserved.

The Supreme Court did not address Lincoln's revocation of habeas corpus until the war had ended. With the writ suspended, a man in the North who had conspired against the country was tried before a military commission rather than in civil court. The tribunal sentenced him to death. Civil war enthusiast Gordon Kwok explains what followed: "The appeal dragged on to 1866, and by then, the war and the national emergency were long over. The need to hang traitors did not exist anymore and in fact, people wanted to forget this horrible war episode and it would be politically incorrect to carry out the sentence." In its ruling, *Ex parte Milligan,* the Supreme Court proclaimed that even though the country was at war, military tribunals should not have been implemented in free states where regular courts were operational. The Court noted that the framers had strived to guard "the foundations of civil liberty against the abuses of unlimited power.... The lessons of history informed them that a trial by an established court, assisted by an impartial jury, was the only sure way of protecting the citizen against oppression and wrong." In overturning Milligan's death sentence, the Supreme Court suggested that it was willing to preserve citizens' liberties once the danger of war had passed.

Civil liberties were curtailed again during World War I, most notably free speech rights. Aaron Delwiche, an assistant professor of communication, describes the sentiment of Americans as they faced war with Germany in 1917:

More than 8 million German-Americans lived in this country, and many were sympathetic to the cause of their homeland. Meanwhile, anti-German feeling was strong among the upper classes on the Atlantic coast. . . . Most Americans, however, were . . . not interested in waging war overseas. The absence of public unity was a primary concern when America entered the war on April 6, 1917. In Washington, unwavering public support was considered to be crucial to the entire wartime effort.

Congress, apprehensive about citizens sympathizing with the Central Powers, passed the Espionage Act of 1917. The law stipulated a $10,000 fine and twenty years in jail for anyone who intentionally interfered with the operation of the military or promoted the success of America's enemies. A year later the Sedition Act criminalized criticism of the government, including "disloyal, scurrilous, and abusive language about the form of government of the United States" and language intended to "incite, provoke, and encourage resistance to the United States."

Many people were prosecuted under these laws during and after the war. One case involved Eugene Debs, a labor leader who gave a public speech in Ohio condemning capitalism and World War I. In his address he lauded socialism and told workers that they were "fit for something better than slavery and cannon fodder." For violating the Espionage Act, he was sentenced to ten years in prison, a punishment that the Supreme Court unanimously affirmed in *Debs v. United States* (1919). Less than a year later a similar case, *Abrams v. United States,* landed in the Court. Five people had distributed antiwar leaflets criticizing capitalism and urging factory workers to strike. Their punishment was twenty years' imprisonment. Again, the Court upheld the defendants' convictions on the basis that their ideas endangered the country in an already perilous time.

Civil liberties concerns resurfaced in subsequent wars, most recently the War on Terror. After America was attacked on September 11, 2001, the military detained hundreds of people, mostly foreigners, suspected of having ties to terrorism. None were immediately charged with a crime and therefore none could contest the allegations against them. This, according to the government, was the best way to keep dangerous criminals from being released to fight against the United States. It rationalized that because most of the detainees were illegal aliens or were citizens captured on foreign battlefields, they should not be accorded the same rights U.S. citizens enjoy. Furthermore, authorities declined to release the names of suspects who had been transferred to a naval base in Guantánamo Bay, Cuba. Doing so, officials argued, would violate the prisoners' privacy and could compromise national security. Meanwhile, the military interrogated the detainees without giving them access to a lawyer. As justification, authorities claimed that the questioning provided useful intelligence on terrorist activities that has helped thwart further strikes. Despite these reassurances, concerned citizens protest that the detainees' right to an attorney, to a hearing, and to refute the charges against them are being grossly violated. Moreover, critics charge that because the prisoners are held in secret, human rights abuses such as torture may take place with impunity.

Initially the Supreme Court rejected appeals on behalf of the terror suspects. It also turned down a case filed by civil liberties groups asserting that the government must turn over information regarding more than one thousand detainees. Lamenting that the Court's refusal to get involved indicated an implicit approval of the government's actions, some people observed that even the Supreme Court's silence can have repercussions on civil liberties.

Nearly three years after September 11, the Court addressed some of these concerns. In *Hamdi v. Rumsfeld* (2004), it confirmed that American citizens suspected of fighting against the country have a right to a hearing, but it also lowered the normal standard for due process. For instance, it specified that the hearing may take place before a military tribunal rather than a civilian court judge, which raised questions about the neutrality of military commissions. Another case in the Supreme Court involves a U.S. citizen, Jose Padilla, who had been imprisoned without charge for three years and was finally indicted on terror-related charges in November 2005. At press time the country was awaiting a ruling in the case, which observers hope will clarify whether and under what circumstances traitorous citizens may be held without trial.

Clearly, the Supreme Court holds much influence over the state of civil liberties in times of national emergency. Sometimes affirming rights and sometimes restricting them, the Court's wartime decisions have set precedents that have stood for years. This anthology examines four significant cases: *Schenck v. United States* (1919), *Korematsu v. United States* (1944), *New York Times Co. v. United States* (1971), and *Hamdi v. Rumsfeld* (2004). Analyzing wartime court decisions can reveal the government's arduous task of balancing national defense measures against citizens' rights. With hope, officials can work to prevent civil liberties infringements in the future while averting danger from enemy forces.

CHAPTER 1

Suppressing Speech That Poses a Clear and Present Danger

Case Overview

Charles T. Schenck v. United States (1919)

In 1918 Charles Schenck, general secretary of the American Socialist Party, caused a commotion that culminated in the first important Supreme Court case involving freedom of speech. He mailed fifteen thousand circulars to men who had been drafted to serve in World War I urging them to oppose the conscription. Forcing men into the military, the pamphlet said, was in violation of the constitutional prohibition of involuntary servitude. Those who stood silent regarding the conscription law, it maintained, were neglecting to assert their rights and were "helping to condone and support a most infamous and insidious conspiracy to abridge and destroy the sacred and cherished rights of a free people." After advising, "Do not submit to intimidation," the pamphlet persuaded readers to petition for the repeal of the draft law. A year earlier, though, Congress had approved the Federal Espionage Act, which forbade attempts to obstruct the recruitment of men into the military. In order to aid the military effort, similar legislation had also outlawed speech that disrespected the government, the Constitution, the flag, or military uniforms.

Upon learning of the Socialist Party's pamphlets, authorities charged Schenck and another party member, Elizabeth Baer, with conspiring to obstruct military recruitment and to cause insubordination in the military. Since the government believed that opposition to the draft could undermine the war effort and endanger the nation, it demanded that such protest be suppressed. Schenck responded that the law violated his First Amendment right to voice his views about the war and the draft. When Schenck was convicted of contravening the Espionage Act and sentenced to six months' imprisonment, he appealed. This would be an important battle pitting the government's need to win the war against the rights of citizens to assert their opinions.

Justice Oliver Wendell Holmes expressed the opinion of the Supreme Court in the case. According to Holmes, Schenck's protests posed a "clear and present danger" to the United States. To illustrate, he offered an example of a man who falsely shouts "fire" in a crowded theater, causing mayhem. Such a person, he suggested, would not be within his constitutional right to free expression; Schenck overstepped his rights in a similar manner when he encouraged insubordination among draftees. Critics of the ruling, however, call this example irrelevant; they counter that Schenck did not make false statements but merely expressed a personal opinion and informed men of their constitutional right to refuse to serve in the military.

The crux of the Court's decision was that the First Amendment is not absolute. More importantly, the ruling offered a test that could be used to determine under what circumstances speech could be muzzled. *Schenck's* clear and present danger formula was utilized to uphold convictions in subsequent free speech cases, including *Debs v. United States* (1919) and *Gitlow v. New York* (1925). In fact, the test was used so often that Holmes later expressed concern that it was being abused and misapplied.

Although *Schenck* was never overturned, its formula was eventually modified. *Brandenburg v. Ohio* (1969) limited the clear and present danger test, making punishable only the advocacy of violent actions, not mere ideas. The Court's opinion in *Schenck v. United States* and the cases that ensued illustrate the continuing conflict between free expression and governmental responsibilities during wartime.

| "Many things that might be said in time of peace ... will not be endured so long as men fight."

The Court's Decision: Free Speech Rights Can Be Restricted in Wartime

Oliver Wendell Holmes

In 1919 the Federal Espionage Act, which banned interference in military recruitment among other activities, was upheld in Schenck v. United States. *In the following viewpoint Justice Oliver Wendell Holmes delivers the unanimous opinion of the Court, which said that a person's right to free speech does not extend to views that pose a clear and present danger to the country. Charles Schenck had sent antiwar leaflets encouraging men to oppose the draft during World War I. Such speech may be acceptable in peacetime, observes Holmes, but during war, statements that could hinder the war effort must be stifled. Holmes served on the Supreme Court from 1902 to 1932.*

This is an indictment in three counts. The first charges a conspiracy to violate the Espionage Act of June 15, 1917, by causing and attempting to cause insubordination in the military and naval forces of the United States, and to obstruct the recruiting and enlistment service of the United States, when the United States was at war with the German Empire, to-wit, that the defendant wilfully conspired to have printed and circulated to men who had been called and accepted for military service under the Act of May 18, 1917, a document set forth and alleged to be calculated to cause such insubordi-

Oliver Wendell Holmes, unanimous opinion, *Schenck v. United States*, 249 U.S. 47, March 13, 1919.

nation and obstruction. The count alleges overt acts in pursuance of the conspiracy, ending in the distribution of the document set forth. The second count alleges a conspiracy to commit an offense against the United States, to-wit, to use the mails for the transmission of matter declared to be nonmailable by title 12, 2, of the Act of June 15, 1917, to-wit, the above mentioned document, with an averment of the same overt acts. The third count charges an unlawful use of the mails for the transmission of the same matter and otherwise as above. The defendants [Charles Schenck and Elizabeth Baer] were found guilty on all the counts. They set up the First Amendment to the Constitution forbidding Congress to make any law abridging the freedom of speech, or of the press, and bringing the case here on that ground have argued some other points also of which we must dispose.

Evidence Against Schenck

It is argued that the evidence, if admissible, was not sufficient to prove that the defendant Schenck was concerned in sending the documents. According to the testimony Schenck said he was general secretary of the Socialist party and had charge of the Socialist headquarters from which the documents were sent. He identified a book found there as the minutes of the Executive Committee of the party. The book showed a resolution of August 13, 1917, that 15,000 leaflets should be printed on the other side of one of them in use, to be mailed to men who had passed exemption boards, and for distribution. Schenck personally attended to the printing. On August 20 the general secretary's report said 'Obtained new leaflets from printer and started work addressing envelopes'; and there was a resolve that Comrade Schenck be allowed $125 for sending leaflets through the mail. He said that he had about fifteen or sixteen thousand printed. There were files of the circular in question in the inner office which he said were printed on the other side of the one sided circular and were there for distribution. Other copies were proved to have been sent through the mails to drafted men. Without going into confirmatory details that were proved, no reasonable man could doubt that the defendant Schenck was largely instrumental in sending the circulars about. As to the defendant Baer there was evidence that she was a member of the Executive Board and that the minutes of its transactions were hers. The argument as to the sufficiency of the evidence that the defendants conspired to send the documents only impairs the seriousness of the real defence.

It is objected that the documentary evidence was not admissible because obtained upon a search warrant, valid so far as appears. The contrary is established. The search warrant did not issue against the defendant but against the Socialist headquarters at 1326 Arch street and it would seem that the documents technically were not even in the defendants' possession. Notwithstanding some protest in argument the notion that evidence even directly proceeding from the defendant in a criminal proceeding is excluded in all cases by the Fifth Amendment is plainly unsound.

The document in question upon its first printed side recited the first section of the Thirteenth Amendment, said that the idea embodied in it was violated by the conscription act and that a conscript is little better than a convict. In impassioned language it intimated that conscription was despotism in its worst form and a monstrous wrong against humanity in the interest of Wall Street's chosen few. It said, 'Do not submit to intimidation,' but in form at least confined itself to peaceful measures such as a petition for the repeal of the act. The other and later printed side of the sheet was headed 'Assert Your Rights.' It stated reasons for alleging that any one violated the Constitution when he refused to recognize 'your right to assert your opposition to the draft,' and went on, 'If you do not assert and support your rights, you are helping to deny or disparage rights which it is the solemn duty of all citizens and residents of the United States to retain.' It described the arguments on the other side as coming from cunning politicians and a mercenary capitalist press, and even silent consent to the conscription law as helping to support an infamous conspiracy. It denied the power to send our citizens away to foreign shores to shoot up the people of other lands, and added that words could not express the condemnation such cold-blooded ruthlessness deserves, winding up, 'You must do your share to maintain, support and uphold the rights of the people of this country.' Of course the document would not have been sent unless it had been intended to have some effect, and we do not see what effect it could be expected to have upon persons subject to the draft except to influence them to obstruct the carrying of it out. The defendants do not deny that the jury might find against them on this point.

Clear and Present Danger

But it is said, suppose that that was the tendency of this circular, it is protected by the First Amendment to the Constitution. Two of the strongest expressions are said to be quoted respectively from well-known public men. It well may be that the prohibition of laws abridging the freedom of speech is not confined to previous restraints, although to prevent them may have been the main purpose, as intimated in *Patterson v. Colorado*. We admit that in many places and in ordinary times the defendants in saying all that was said in the circular would have been within their constitutional rights. But the character of every act depends upon the circumstances in which it is done. The most stringent protection of free speech would not protect a man in falsely shouting fire in a theatre and causing a panic. It does not even protect a man from an injunction against uttering words that may have all the effect of force. The question in every case is whether the words used are used in such circumstances and are of such a nature as to create a clear and present danger that they will bring about the substantive evils that Congress has a right to prevent. It is a question of proximity and degree. When a nation is at war many things that might be said in time of peace are such a hindrance to its effort that their utterance will not be endured so long as men fight and that no Court could regard them as protected by any constitutional right. It seems to be admitted that if an actual obstruction of the recruiting service were proved, liability for words that produced that effect might be enforced. The statute of 1917 in section 4 punishes conspiracies to obstruct as well as actual obstruction. If the act, (speaking, or circulating a paper,) its tendency and the intent with which it is done are the same, we perceive no ground for saying that success alone warrants making the act a crime. Indeed that case might be said to dispose of the present contention if the precedent covers all media. But as the right to free speech was not referred to specially, we have thought fit to add a few words.

It was not argued that a conspiracy to obstruct the draft was not within the words of the Act of 1917. The words are 'obstruct the recruiting or enlistment service,' and it might be suggested that they refer only to making it hard to get volunteers. Recruiting heretofore usually having been accomplished by getting volunteers the word is apt to call up that method only in our minds. But recruiting is gaining fresh supplies for the forces, as well by draft as otherwise. It is put as an alternative to enlistment or voluntary enrollment in this act. The fact that the Act of 1917 was enlarged by the amending Act of May 16, 1918, of course, does not affect the present indictment and would not, even if the former act had been repealed.

Judgments affirmed.

> "*[Constitutional] protection is not extended ... as a cover for unchecked efforts to overthrow our theory of government.*"

Schenck Confirms That the Right to Free Speech Is Not Absolute

George W. Wickersham

George W. Wickersham, who was attorney general under President William Taft, asserts in the following viewpoint that the First Amendment right to free speech and assembly must sometimes be limited. Writing shortly after Schenck v. United States *(1919) and similar decisions in which people were convicted for criticizing the government, Wickersham opines that World War I–era sedition laws were necessary to prevent subversion. With the country still unsettled following the war, he maintains, violent crimes and further destruction could result if people are permitted to speak against the government. Wickersham wrote this viewpoint in response to a letter sent by the* Nation *to a group of lawyers. It charged that people, particularly foreigners, were denied their rights to free speech and assembly during and immediately following the war.*

So far as the violation by the police of the right of assembly and parade is concerned, the matter seems to have been disposed of in the proper legal fashion by the magistrate before whom the persons arrested by the police were taken. As to the prohibition against assembly in different parts of the country, each instance depends, I assume, upon a particular state of facts. There seems to be no doubt that a very large

George W. Wickersham, letter to the *Nation*, April 17, 1920.

number of foreigners who have been enjoying the protection of American laws are actively engaged in endeavoring to subvert the institutions of this country, and to substitute by various unlawful means the form of government which is popularly known as 'Soviet' for the constitutional government established by our institutions. The activities of these people are varied, and I should not get very much excited over the question of preventing them from meeting and shouting themselves hoarse over their particular projects, were it not that, in the present unsettled condition following the war, foolish vaporings, which, under ordinary circumstances, would have no other effect than to gratify the speakers, result in crimes of violence and destruction of property. There is no absolute right of free speech, despite the language of the First Amendment of the Constitution. As Judge [Oliver Wendell] Holmes said, in delivering the opinion of the Supreme Court in a recent case [*Schenck v. United States* (1919)]:

> The most stringent protection of free speech would not protect a man in falsely shouting fire in a theater and causing a panic. It does not even protect a man from an injunction against uttering words that may have all the effect of force. . . . The question in every case is whether the words used are used in such circumstances and are of such a nature as to create a clear and present danger that they will bring about the substantive evils that Congress has a right to prevent. It is a question of proximity and degree. When a nation is at war many things that might be said in time of peace are such a hindrance to its effort that their utterance will not be endured so long as men fight and that no Court could regard them as protected by any constitutional right.

Dissenters Crippled the War Effort

In a modified degree, the same rule applies to the anomalous period of technical war and partial social demoralization through which we are now passing. It may be that this is resented by the labor audiences. . . . I am inclined to think that these audiences are made up, or at all events their complexion is colored, by the class of agitators to whom I have referred. The methods of repression by the police are not apt to be gentle; they often are brutal; they call for severe condemnation; but in dealing with them, the particular instance must be borne in mind. The fact that individual policemen in scattered localities are harsh in enforcing the law does not justify a conclusion that the law should be repealed. I do not think it was on any such issue of liberty as this that [Benjamin] Franklin, [Thomas] Jefferson, [John] Adams, and a host of our forefathers lifted up their voices; at least, I am unacquainted with any history that would justify that conclusion. The fact is that the principal complaints, so far as I am familiar with them, have come from the class of people who used such influence as they had in every possible way to prevent the United States from taking its part in preventing Germany from extending her militaristic system of government over the world, and in crippling, so far as they might, the effectiveness of our efforts when we did join the war. I am inclined to think that a wholesome lesson will be taught if the foreigners who have come here and enjoyed the protection of our laws shall learn that that protection is not extended to them as a cover for unchecked efforts to overthrow our theory of government or our conception of civilization.

> "The proper response of the government should not be to prohibit dissent, but to protect the speaker."

Free Speech Rights Should Be Preserved in Wartime

Geoffrey R. Stone, interviewed by Ronald K.L. Collins

Geoffrey R. Stone, law professor and author of Perilous Times: Free Speech in Wartime, *is interviewed in the following viewpoint by First Amendment Center scholar Ronald K.L. Collins. According to Stone, World War I–era legislation that banned seditious expression, under which antiwar activists such as Charles Schenck were prosecuted, resulted in grave rights violations. Not only did the acts attempt to silence dissent, Stone claims, but they were used as justification for beating and even killing protesters. Instead of controlling speech, Stone proposes, the government should work to guarantee wide discourse even in times of war. To this end, Stone lauds Supreme Court justice Oliver Wendell Holmes, who wrote the opinion upholding Schenck's conviction, for gradually adjusting his views and defending the freedom of expression in later cases.*

Ronald Collins: *If you were to pick one or two core insights that came to you in the course of writing* Perilous Times, *what would they be?*

Geoffrey Stone: First, democracy is always a work in progress. We can never be complacent about our liberties. Just as we are now trying very self-consciously to build a culture of democracy in Iraq, so too must we constantly reaffirm and reinvent American democracy. When the people stop thinking about their rights—and the rights of others—all is lost. An important goal of *Perilous Times* is to contribute to that ongoing process of national self-discovery and reaffirmation.

Second, we learn from experience. We learn unevenly, but we do learn. We have a stronger culture of respect for civil liberties today than we've ever had before. I was surprised to come to this conclusion. Of course, our commitment to civil liberties is always contingent, always somewhat fragile, and as *Perilous Times* reveals, a culture of respect for civil liberties can easily be overwhelmed by the fears and anxieties of wartime.

In the introduction to your book, you write: "In order to understand free speech, we must understand free speech in wartime." Could you explain that a bit more for our readers?

In working on the book, I was surprised to discover something I'd never before realized: The United States government has never attempted directly to suppress criticism of public policies or public officials except in time of war. (Perhaps everyone else had figured this out before me, but I don't think so.) Except in the episodes addressed in *Perilous Times* (the near war with France in 1798, the Civil War, World War I, World War II, the Cold War and the Vietnam War), the federal government has stayed out of the business of punishing people for "seditious" expression. That's an important and revealing insight. . . .

Heroes and Villains

Was Justice Oliver Wendell Holmes more of a hero or villain in the history of free speech? After the rule and application of Schenck—*followed in* Abrams, Frohwerk, Debs, *and* Gilbert—*it took almost a half-century to undo* Schenck's *doctrinal harm. And even so,* Schenck *survives, in a formal sense, as a precedent if only because* Brandenburg v. Ohio *(1969) is not a wartime case, and* Schenck *has never been explicitly overruled. Given that, what should we make of Holmes and his handiwork, both in terms of what he said and did?*

As [First Amendment scholar] Harry Kalven once observed, Justice Holmes "got off to a rather limping start" in his eventual role as the great defender of free speech with his 1919 opinion in *Schenck*. Nonetheless, Holmes, along with Justices [Louis] Brandeis, [Hugo] Black, [William] Douglas and [William] Brennan, is one of the judicial heroes of the First Amendment.

To me, the most interesting thing about Holmes's evolution is that it illustrates quite powerfully the very idea that was at issue. That is, with continued debate and deliberation, Holmes learned. The progression of his views on free speech from *Schenck* to *Abrams* to *Gitlow* demonstrates the power of the "marketplace of ideas."

Ultimately, Holmes had more influence on both the constitutional and public understandings of the First Amendment than any other figure in American history. The closing paragraph of his dissenting opinion in *Abrams* remains, in my view, the most eloquent and most moving statement ever written about free speech in the United States....

War and Experiments in Freedom

From a First Amendment perspective, what was the worst "wartime period" in our history and why?

I don't know if I can "rank" these eras with any precision. The circumstances were so different from one period to the next that such measurement is next to impossible.

With that caveat, I would say that from a free-speech perspective the three worst periods were 1798, World War I and the Cold War. In each of these eras, national political leaders intentionally generated a wave of public fear in order to silence their critics.

In 1798, the Federalists used the Sedition Act as a political weapon in an effort to destroy the Republicans and secure victory in the election of 1800. During World War I, the Wilson administration created a propaganda agency, the Commit-

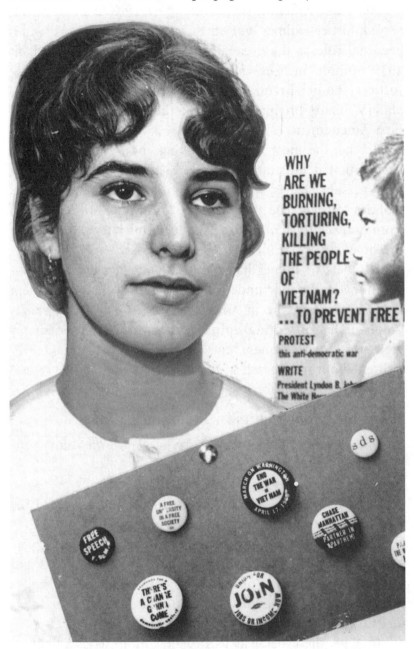

Judy Pardun, a member of Students for a Democratic Society, expresses her right to free speech during wartime in protest of the Vietnam War. Library of Congress

tee on Public Information, in order to propagate the view that anti-war dissent was treasonable. And during the Cold War, Republicans exploited anti-communist hysteria in a partisan effort to regain control of the national government. In each of these episodes, anyone who expressed nonconforming views ran a serious risk of persecution and/or prosecution. . . .

In some circumstances, dissenters act lawfully, but their opponents respond with violence. Too often, government has taken the view that to prevent such violence it must silence the dissenter. This was frequently the case during World War I, for example. Indeed, the Sedition Act of 1918, which made it unlawful for any person to utter or publish any disloyal, scurrilous, or abusive views about the government, the flag, or the Constitution, was "justified" by its supporters as a means of preventing violence against dissenters, some of whom had been severely beaten and even hanged by self-proclaimed "patriots." This is perverse.

The Rights of Protesters

The proper response of the government should not be to prohibit dissent, but to protect the speaker and punish those who resort to violence. The very idea of a "heckler's veto" (that is, allowing a speaker's opponents to cause the speaker's arrest by threatening violence) is incompatible with the most basic premises of the First Amendment. The Supreme Court finally came to this conclusion during the civil rights movement of the 1960s. . . .

Certainly, a dissenter has a First Amendment right to urge others to sign anti-war petitions and participate in anti-war demonstrations. But does she have a right to urge others to protest the war by blowing up buildings? This question has long haunted the Supreme Court, and it recurs throughout *Perilous Times*.

In 1969, the Court held in *Brandenburg* that a speaker cannot constitutionally be punished even for advocacy of law violation unless violence is likely to occur imminently. This may be the best measure of how much risk we are prepared to run in order to preserve a broad range of free speech. As it turns out, after two centuries of doctrinal evolution, we are willing to accept quite a bit of risk in order to guarantee a robust and wide-open political discourse, even in time of war. Essentially, the Supreme Court has concluded that, except in true emergencies, the government must focus its energy on punishing the lawbreaker rather than silencing the speaker.

"The Court could apply the [Schenck] test not only to restrict speech, but also to protect it."

Applying the Clear and Present Danger Test to Future Cases

R. Bruce Carroll

In this selection R. Bruce Carroll discusses the implications of the formula developed in Schenck v. United States *(1919) in which speech can be suppressed if it poses a clear and present danger to the government. Carroll asserts that Justice Oliver Wendell Holmes, writing the Court's opinion in* Schenck, *intended for the test to establish narrow grounds on which speech can be restricted. However, Carroll notes, the Court applied this formula more broadly in later cases, consistently curbing speech more readily than Holmes intended. R. Bruce Carroll edited* The Constitutional Literacy Reader, *from which the following viewpoint is excerpted.*

The First Amendment freedoms of speech, religion, press, and assembly have never been interpreted by a majority of the Supreme Court as absolute. Since some regulation of these rights is constitutional, the Court has constantly been confronted with the task of deciding just how much. In the process it has had to attempt to balance individual liberties against the rights and needs of society to regulate and protect those liberties. It is clear, for example, that freedom of speech would extend to shouting "Fire!" in a vacant meadow: it is also clear that it would not extend to a person's shouting

R. Bruce Carroll, ed., *The Constitutional Literacy Reader,* Federal Executive Institute and Management Development Centers. www.leadership.opm.gov.

"Fire!" in a crowded theater when there was no fire and when the result could be a stampede for the exits that endangered all. The question becomes one of time, place, and circumstance for determination of the extent to which one may exercise First Amendment freedoms. . . .

The Clear and Present Danger Test

Perhaps the most famous test to determine impermissible speech that the Court has used is the "clear and present danger" test. This test says that when men use speech in such a way as to create an immediate danger that substantive evils will follow, against which society has a right to protect itself through legislation, then the words themselves may be declared unlawful and those who utter them punished. Substantive evils are those inimical to the security and welfare of society which the legislature specifies as crimes.

This test originated in 1919, when Justice [Oliver Wendell] Holmes for a unanimous court in the case of *Schenck v. U.S.* used the words "clear and present danger" to justify legislation which patently suppressed speech. This case arose during World War I, an era of "Red Scares," bombings, and allegedly Communist-inspired labor strikes, and a time when great fear of a socio-economic revolution gripped the American public.

Schenck had transmitted a circular through the mails which urged those eligible for the draft to oppose it. The circular labelled the draft despotism in its worst form and advocated insubordination upon entrance into the armed forces. He was indicted for violating the Espionage Act of 1917, which penalized actions and speech designed to "interfere with the prosecution of the war." Justice Holmes did not question whether the provisions of the Espionage Act were "reasonable" limitations upon the right of free speech; rather, he sought to determine the proximity and degree of Schenck's actions and words to those made unlawful by the act.

The question in every case is whether the words used are used in such circumstance and are of such a nature as to create a clear and present danger that they will bring about the substantive evils that Congress has a right to prevent. It is a question of proximity and degree.

Holmes continued by noting that the "character of every act depends upon the circumstances in which it is done." Here, "when a nation is at war many things that might be said in time of peace are such a hindrance to its effort that their utterance will not be endured so long as men fight and that no Court could regard them as protected by any constitutional right." It is speech that may be prevented, not just action, for "if the act, its tendency and the intent with which it is done are the same, there is ... no ground for saying that success alone warrants making the act a crime." Holmes assumed that the intent of the document was obstruction within the meaning of the Act.

> Of course the document would not have been sent unless it had been intended to have some effect, and we do not see what effect it could be expected to have upon persons subject to the draft except to influence them to obstruct the carrying of it out.

Thus, it seems that while formulating what was to become the standard for cases of this kind, Holmes was actually deciding the case on grounds of intent rather than the existence or absence of a "clear and present danger."

Schenck as Precedent

The effect of *Schenck* was to give judicial blessing to legislative attempts to restrict speech in the name of national security. It created a general rule for determining when speech may be restricted—when words are in such proximity to illegal acts and of such a degree as to urge or incite such illegal acts so as to constitute a clear and present danger to the state. It clearly established that the First Amendment freedoms are not absolute; they may be restricted in special circumstances. Above

all, it set a standard subject to the vagaries of the Court because of the number of central questions it left to subsequent
determination and discretion. What is a *clear* and *present* danger? How *proximate* must the words be to the illegal act? To
what *degree* must the words urge the prohibited act? What is
the *character* of the words in relation to the circumstances in
which they were uttered that is proscribed? What constitute a
threat to national security? These and other questions placed
the Court in the position of having to interpret the constitutionality of law relative to the facts and circumstances of each
case. In that effort the Court could apply the test not only to
restrict speech, but also to protect it.

That Holmes viewed his opinion as creating a new judicial
standard is not apparent. One week after the *Schenck* case,
Holmes again wrote for a unanimous Court in *Frowerk v. U.S.*
and *Debs v. U.S.* Upholding convictions again under the Espionage Act, the Court cited *Schenck* as analogous, but did not
refer explicitly to the clear and present danger test. The cases
set the stage for the next Espionage Act conviction which
came to the Court in *Abrams v. U.S.*

The Espionage Act had been amended in 1918 to include
within its proscriptions advocating reduction of production of
war materials with the intent of hindering the prosecution of
the war. This addition constituted a direct regulation of speech
as speech, not just speech as it related to conduct, and only
intent needed to be proved to violate it. While the nation was
involved in World War I, the defendants were convicted under
the act of unlawfully writing and publishing language "intended to incite, provoke and encourage resistance to /and
criticism of/ the United States" and conspiring "to urge, incite
and advocate curtailment of production of ordnance and am-
munition necessary and essential to the prosecution of war."

Their conviction was upheld by the Supreme Court. Justice [Tom] Clark wrote for the majority that although appel-
lants were interested primarily in aiding the Russian Revolu-

tion, they "must be held to have intended, and to be accountable for, the effects which their acts were likely to produce." These effects included hindering the war effort; therefore, the majority held them within the reach of the statute. Although relying upon the *Schenck* case as precedent, the Court did not mention the clear and present danger test.

The *Schenck* Formula Protects Free Speech

The conviction generated one of the most famous Holmes dissents in which Justice [Louis] Brandeis concurred. [He asserted,] "Only the emergency that makes it immediately dangerous to leave the correction of evil counsels to time warrants making any exception to the sweeping command, 'Congress shall make no law abridging freedom of speech.'" [Although Holmes wrote,] "We should be eternally vigilant against attempts to check the expression of opinions that we loathe and believe to be fraught with death, unless they so imminently threaten immediate interference with the lawful and pressing purposes of the law that an immediate check is required to save the country," surely that is not the case here. Since Abrams' intent was not to obstruct war production in order to hinder the war, he could not have created a clear and present danger. No such danger could be created by "the surreptitious publishing of a silly leaflet by an unknown man." [Holmes continued,]

> . . . when men have realized that time has upset many fighting faiths, they may come to believe even more than they believe the very foundations of their own conduct that the ultimate good desired is better reached by free-trade in ideas —that the best test of truth is the power of the thought to get itself accepted in the competition of the market. . . .

Thus, for Holmes, speech could be restricted, but only when "lawful and pressing" purposes of the law are so "imminently" threatened as to imperil the safety of the nation. The clear and present danger test could be used only on very narrow grounds as a justification for limiting the right to free speech.

In *Schaefer v. U.S.* (1919), an Espionage Act case involving statements published in two newspapers concerning the war, Brandeis with Holmes dissented. After quoting the *Schenck* clear and present danger formulation, they stated the test is a rule of reason: "Correctly applied, it will preserve the right of free speech both from suppression by tyrannous, well-meaning majorities and from abuse by irresponsible, fanatical minorities." And in *Pierce v. U.S.*, again Holmes quoted his *Schenck* formula and argued that its requirements had not been met, although the majority as in *Schaefer* relied upon it to uphold convictions. While the majority of the Court was using the new formula for restricting speech, its creator was dissenting on the ground that the majority was improperly applying it.

CHAPTER 2

Upholding the Evacuation of Japanese Americans

Case Overview

Toyosaburo Korematsu v. United States (1944)

In February 1942 President Franklin Roosevelt signed an executive order that led to the forced relocation of over 100,000 citizens and aliens of Japanese ancestry. Following Japan's attack on Pearl Harbor, Hawaii, in December 1941, the U.S. government had begun to suspect Japanese Americans of signaling enemy ships from the West Coast, which was a military area. Unable to quickly identify which Japanese Americans posed a threat, the military ordered all people of Japanese blood to evacuate the West Coast states and southern Arizona and enter internment camps. Leaving behind their homes, businesses, and other property, the evacuees moved to relocation centers surrounded by barbed wire and armed sentries. Offering unfurnished barracks with communal latrines and little privacy, the centers were called concentration camps by some people.

One American citizen of Japanese descent, however, refused to leave his home near Oakland, California. It was unfair, thought Fred Korematsu, that loyal citizens should be sent away simply because of their race. Consequently, he changed his name and underwent eyelid surgery in order to appear less Japanese. Eventually he was caught and convicted of violating military orders. Although Korematsu's allegiance to the United States was never in question, he was sent to a relocation camp.

Korematsu appealed his case in 1944 to the Supreme Court, where his attorneys accused the government of illegally detaining Americans without a hearing or trial. While the Court conceded that "compulsory exclusion of large groups of citizens from their homes . . . is inconsistent with our basic governmental institutions," it determined the action was acceptable because the country was at war. In a 6-3 decision, the

Court upheld Korematsu's conviction, signifying that when the country is threatened by hostile forces, its leaders may restrict civil liberties in order to protect national security. Writing separately in their dissents, Justice Frank Murphy called the decision a "legalization of racism," and Justice Robert Jackson protested: "Here is an attempt to make an otherwise innocent act a crime merely because this prisoner . . . belongs to a race from which there is no way to resign."

When federal district court judge Marilyn Patel reviewed the *Korematsu* case in 1983, she learned that the government's assertions about Japanese spies were based on unsubstantiated claims and racist beliefs. Accordingly, Judge Patel vacated Korematsu's conviction. The original decision, she declared, stands as a reminder that in time of war "our institutions must be vigilant in protecting constitutional guarantees." *Korematsu* has been cited in recent War on Terror cases, including *Hamdi v. Rumsfeld* (2004), which found that even citizens who engaged in armed conflict against the United States must not be detained without receiving a hearing.

> "Exclusion [of Japanese Americans] from
> a threatened area ... has a definite and
> close relationship to the prevention of es-
> pionage."

The Court's Decision: The Mass Evacuation of Japanese Americans Is Justified

Hugo Black

*During World War II aliens and citizens of Japanese descent
were forced to leave the West Coast of the United States and re-
locate to internment camps. According to Justice Hugo Black in
the following excerpt from the Supreme Court's decision in* Korematsu v. United States, *the compulsory evacuation was necessary to prevent espionage by Japanese Americans who remained
loyal to Japan. In wartime, the Court contends, the military has
the authority to decide who may or may not remain in areas
threatened by attack (such as the West Coast area). Moreover,
the restrictions placed on the civil liberties of some citizens were
defensible, the Court asserts, because they were intended to preserve national security in a time of war. Hugo Black was a Supreme Court justice from 1937 to 1971.*

The petitioner, an American citizen of Japanese descent, was convicted in a federal district court for remaining in San Leandro, California, a "Military Area," contrary to Civilian Exclusion Order No. 34 of the Commanding General of the Western Command, U.S. Army, which directed that, after May 9, 1942, all persons of Japanese ancestry should be excluded from that area. No question was raised as to petitioner's loy-

Hugo Black, majority opinion, *Korematsu v. United States,* 323 U.S. 214, December 18, 1944.

alty to the United States. The Circuit Court of Appeals affirmed, and the importance of the constitutional question involved caused us to grant certiorari.

It should be noted, to begin with, that all legal restrictions which curtail the civil rights of a single racial group are immediately suspect. That is not to say that all such restrictions are unconstitutional. It is to say that courts must subject them to the most rigid scrutiny. Pressing public necessity may sometimes justify the existence of such restrictions; racial antagonism never can.

Exclusion Order No. 34

In the instant case, prosecution of the petitioner was begun by information charging violation of an Act of Congress, of March 21, 1942, 56 Stat. 173, which provides that

> ... whoever shall enter, remain in, leave, or commit any act in any military area or military zone prescribed, under the authority of an Executive order of the President, by the Secretary of War, or by any military commander designated by the Secretary of War, contrary to the restrictions applicable to any such area or zone or contrary to the order of the Secretary of War or any such military commander, shall, if it appears that he knew or should have known of the existence and extent of the restrictions or order and that his act was in violation thereof, be guilty of a misdemeanor and upon conviction shall be liable to a fine of not to exceed $5,000 or to imprisonment for not more than one year, or both, for each offense.

Exclusion Order No. 34, which the petitioner knowingly and admittedly violated, was one of a number of military orders and proclamations, all of which were substantially based upon Executive Order No. 9066, 7 Fed. Reg. 1407. That order, issued after we were at war with Japan, declared that

> the successful prosecution of the war requires every possible protection against espionage and against sabotage to na-

tional defense material, national defense premises, and national defense utilities. . . .

One of the series of orders and proclamations, a curfew order, which, like the exclusion order here, was promulgated pursuant to Executive Order 9066, subjected all persons of Japanese ancestry in prescribed West Coast military areas to remain in their residences from 8 P.M. to 6 A.M. As is the case with the exclusion order here, that prior curfew order was designed as a "protection against espionage and against sabotage." In *Hirabayashi v. United States,* we sustained a conviction obtained for violation of the curfew order. The *Hirabayashi* conviction and this one thus rest on the same 1942 Congressional Act and the same basic executive and military orders, all of which orders were aimed at the twin dangers of espionage and sabotage.

The War Powers of Congress

The 1942 Act was attacked in the *Hirabayashi* case as an unconstitutional delegation of power; it was contended that the curfew order and other orders on which it rested were beyond the war powers of the Congress, the military authorities, and of the President, as Commander in Chief of the Army, and, finally, that to apply the curfew order against none but citizens of Japanese ancestry amounted to a constitutionally prohibited discrimination solely on account of race. To these questions, we gave the serious consideration which their importance justified. We upheld the curfew order as an exercise of the power of the government to take steps necessary to prevent espionage and sabotage in an area threatened by Japanese attack.

In the light of the principles we announced in the *Hirabayashi* case, we are unable to conclude that it was beyond the war power of Congress and the Executive to exclude those of Japanese ancestry from the West Coast war area at the time they did. True, exclusion from the area in which one's home is located is a far greater deprivation than constant confinement to the home from 8 P.M. to 6 A.M. Nothing short of apprehension by the proper military authorities of the gravest imminent danger to the public safety can constitutionally justify either. But exclusion from a threatened area, no less than curfew, has a definite and close relationship to the prevention of espionage and sabotage. The military authorities, charged with the primary responsibility of defending our shores, concluded that curfew provided inadequate protection and ordered exclusion. They did so, as pointed out in our *Hirabayashi* opinion, in accordance with Congressional authority to the military to say who should, and who should not, remain in the threatened areas.

In this case, the petitioner challenges the assumptions upon which we rested our conclusions in the *Hirabayashi* case. He also urges that, by May, 1942, when Order No. 34 was promulgated, all danger of Japanese invasion of the West Coast had disappeared. After careful consideration of these contentions, we are compelled to reject them.

Here, as in the *Hirabayashi* case,

> . . . we cannot reject as unfounded the judgment of the military authorities and of Congress that there were disloyal members of that population, whose number and strength could not be precisely and quickly ascertained. We cannot say that the war-making branches of the Government did not have ground for believing that, in a critical hour, such persons could not readily be isolated and separately dealt with, and constituted a menace to the national defense and safety which demanded that prompt and adequate measures be taken to guard against it.

An Aggregation of Hardships

Like curfew, exclusion of those of Japanese origin was deemed necessary because of the presence of an unascertained number of disloyal members of the group, most of whom we have no

47

doubt were loyal to this country. It was because we could not reject the finding of the military authorities that it was impossible to bring about an immediate segregation of the disloyal from the loyal that we sustained the validity of the curfew order as applying to the whole group. In the instant case, temporary exclusion of the entire group was rested by the military on the same ground. The judgment that exclusion of the whole group was, for the same reason, a military imperative answers the contention that the exclusion was in the nature of group punishment based on antagonism to those of Japanese origin. That there were members of the group who retained loyalties to Japan has been confirmed by investigations made subsequent to the exclusion. Approximately five thousand American citizens of Japanese ancestry refused to swear unqualified allegiance to the United States and to renounce allegiance to the Japanese Emperor, and several thousand evacuees requested repatriation to Japan.

We uphold the exclusion order as of the time it was made and when the petitioner violated it. In doing so, we are not unmindful of the hardships imposed by it upon a large group of American citizens. But hardships are part of war, and war is an aggregation of hardships. All citizens alike, both in and out of uniform, feel the impact of war in greater or lesser measure. Citizenship has its responsibilities, as well as its privileges, and, in time of war, the burden is always heavier. Compulsory exclusion of large groups of citizens from their homes, except under circumstances of direst emergency and peril, is inconsistent with our basic governmental institutions. But when, under conditions of modern warfare, our shores are threatened by hostile forces, the power to protect must be commensurate with the threatened danger. . . .

The Evacuation Order Was Justified

It is said that we are dealing here with the case of imprisonment of a citizen in a concentration camp solely because of his ancestry, without evidence or inquiry concerning his loyalty and good disposition towards the United States. Our task would be simple, our duty clear, were this a case involving the imprisonment of a loyal citizen in a concentration camp because of racial prejudice. Regardless of the true nature of the assembly and relocation centers—and we deem it unjustifiable to call them concentration camps, with all the ugly connotations that term implies—we are dealing specifically with nothing but an exclusion order. To cast this case into outlines of racial prejudice, without reference to the real military dangers which were presented, merely confuses the issue. Korematsu was not excluded from the Military Area because of hostility to him or his race. He was excluded because we are at war with the Japanese Empire, because the properly constituted military authorities feared an invasion of our West Coast and felt constrained to take proper security measures, because they decided that the military urgency of the situation demanded that all citizens of Japanese ancestry be segregated from the West Coast temporarily, and, finally, because Congress, reposing its confidence in this time of war in our military leaders—as inevitably it must—determined that they should have the power to do just this. There was evidence of disloyalty on the part of some, the military authorities considered that the need for action was great, and time was short. We cannot—by availing ourselves of the calm perspective of hindsight—now say that, at that time, these actions were unjustified.

| "Under our system of law, individual guilt
is the sole basis for deprivation of rights."

Dissenting Opinion: The Mass Evacuation of Japanese Americans Is Racist

Frank Murphy

The decision to exclude Japanese Americans from the Pacific Coast during World War II was based on discriminatory beliefs and falsehoods, argues Supreme Court justice Frank Murphy in the following dissent in Korematsu v. United States. *Japanese Americans were removed from their homes not because they were generally disloyal to the United States or were endangered by Americans hostile to them, as has been suggested, but because of long-standing racial and economic prejudices against them, Murphy charges. As a result, he avers, the evacuees' constitutional rights to equal protection and procedural due process were violated. Because the military decree was rooted in racist beliefs, Murphy declares, Fred Korematsu's conviction for not abiding by it is essentially a "legalization of racism." Murphy served on the Supreme Court from 1940 to 1949.*

This exclusion of "all persons of Japanese ancestry, both alien and non-alien," from the Pacific Coast area on a plea of military necessity in the absence of martial law ought not to be approved. Such exclusion goes over "the very brink of constitutional power" and falls into the ugly abyss of racism.

In dealing with matters relating to the prosecution and progress of a war, we must accord great respect and consideration to the judgments of the military authorities who are on the scene and who have full knowledge of the military facts.

Frank Murphy, dissenting opinion, *Korematsu v. United States,* 323 U.S. 214, December 18, 1944.

The scope of their discretion must, as a matter of necessity and common sense, be wide. And their judgments ought not to be overruled lightly by those whose training and duties ill-equip them to deal intelligently with matters so vital to the physical security of the nation.

At the same time, however, it is essential that there be definite limits to military discretion, especially where martial law has not been declared. Individuals must not be left impoverished of their constitutional rights on a plea of military necessity that has neither substance nor support. Thus, like other claims conflicting with the asserted constitutional rights of the individual, the military claim must subject itself to the judicial process of having its reasonableness determined and its conflicts with other interests reconciled.

Immediate, Imminent, and Impending Danger

[As noted in *Sterling v. Constantin*,]

> What are the allowable limits of military discretion, and whether or not they have been overstepped in a particular case, are judicial questions.

The judicial test of whether the Government, on a plea of military necessity, can validly deprive an individual of any of his constitutional rights is whether the deprivation is reasonably related to a public danger that is so "immediate, imminent, and impending" as not to admit of delay and not to permit the intervention of ordinary constitutional processes to alleviate the danger. Civilian Exclusion Order No. 34, banishing from a prescribed area of the Pacific Coast "all persons of Japanese ancestry, both alien and non-alien," clearly does not meet that test. Being an obvious racial discrimination, the order deprives all those within its scope of the equal protection of the laws as guaranteed by the Fifth Amendment. It further deprives these individuals of their constitutional rights to live and work where they will, to establish a home where they choose and to move about freely. In excommunicating them without benefit of hearings, this order also deprives them of all their constitutional rights to procedural due process. Yet no reasonable relation to an "immediate, imminent, and impending" public danger is evident to support this racial restriction which is one of the most sweeping and complete deprivations of constitutional rights in the history of this nation in the absence of martial law.

It must be conceded that the military and naval situation in the spring of 1942 was such as to generate a very real fear of invasion of the Pacific Coast, accompanied by fears of sabotage and espionage in that area. The military command was therefore justified in adopting all reasonable means necessary to combat these dangers. In adjudging the military action taken in light of the then apparent dangers, we must not erect too high or too meticulous standards; it is necessary only that the action have some reasonable relation to the removal of the dangers of invasion, sabotage and espionage. But the exclusion, either temporarily or permanently, of all persons with Japanese blood in their veins has no such reasonable relation. And that relation is lacking because the exclusion order necessarily must rely for its reasonableness upon the assumption that all persons of Japanese ancestry may have a dangerous tendency to commit sabotage and espionage and to aid our Japanese enemy in other ways. It is difficult to believe that reason, logic, or experience could be marshalled in support of such an assumption.

Discriminatory Beliefs

That this forced exclusion was the result in good measure of this erroneous assumption of racial guilt, rather than *bona fide* military necessity is evidenced by the Commanding General's Final Report on the evacuation from the Pacific Coast area. In it, he refers to all individuals of Japanese descent as "subver-

A Japanese American store owner displays this sign reading "I Am an American" in his store window in response to the order that all persons of Japanese descent evacuate from the Pacific Coast. Library of Congress

sive," as belonging to "an enemy race" whose "racial strains are undiluted," and as constituting "over 112,000 potential enemies ... at large today" along the Pacific Coast. In support of this blanket condemnation of all persons of Japanese descent, however, no reliable evidence is cited to show that such individuals were generally disloyal, or had generally so conducted themselves in this area as to constitute a special menace to defense installations or war industries, or had otherwise, by their behavior, furnished reasonable ground for their exclusion as a group.

Justification for the exclusion is sought, instead, mainly upon questionable racial and sociological grounds not ordinarily within the realm of expert military judgment, supplemented by certain semi-military conclusions drawn from an unwarranted use of circumstantial evidence. Individuals of

Japanese ancestry are condemned because they are said [in the Final Report] to be "a large, unassimilated, tightly knit racial group, bound to an enemy nation by strong ties of race, culture, custom and religion." They are claimed to be given to "emperor worshipping ceremonies" and to "dual citizenship." Japanese language schools and allegedly pro-Japanese organizations are cited as evidence of possible group disloyalty, together with facts as to certain persons being educated and residing at length in Japan. It is intimated that many of these individuals deliberately resided "adjacent to strategic points," thus enabling them

> to carry into execution a tremendous program of sabotage on a mass scale should any considerable number of them have been inclined to do so.

The need for protective custody is also asserted. The report refers without identity to "numerous incidents of violence" as well as to other admittedly unverified or cumulative incidents. From this, plus certain other events not shown to have been connected with the Japanese Americans, it is concluded that the "situation was fraught with danger to the Japanese population itself " and that the general public "was ready to take matters into its own hands." Finally, it is intimated, though not directly charged or proved, that persons of Japanese ancestry were responsible for three minor isolated shellings and bombings of the Pacific Coast area, as well as for unidentified radio transmissions and night signaling.

The main reasons relied upon by those responsible for the forced evacuation, therefore, do not prove a reasonable relation between the group characteristics of Japanese Americans and the dangers of invasion, sabotage and espionage. The reasons appear, instead, to be largely an accumulation of much of the misinformation, half-truths and insinuations that for years have been directed against Japanese Americans by people with racial and economic prejudices—the same people who have been among the foremost advocates of the evacuation. A military judgment based upon such racial and sociological considerations is not entitled to the great weight ordinarily given the judgments based upon strictly military considerations. Especially is this so when every charge relative to race, religion, culture, geographical location, and legal and economic status has been substantially discredited by independent studies made by experts in these matters.

Individual Guilt vs. Racial Guilt

The military necessity which is essential to the validity of the evacuation order thus resolves itself into a few intimations that certain individuals actively aided the enemy, from which it is inferred that the entire group of Japanese Americans could not be trusted to be or remain loyal to the United States. No one denies, of course, that there were some disloyal persons of Japanese descent on the Pacific Coast who did all in their power to aid their ancestral land. Similar disloyal activities have been engaged in by many persons of German, Italian and even more pioneer stock in our country. But to infer that examples of individual disloyalty prove group disloyalty and justify discriminatory action against the entire group is to deny that, under our system of law, individual guilt is the sole basis for deprivation of rights. Moreover, this inference, which is at the very heart of the evacuation orders, has been used in support of the abhorrent and despicable treatment of minority groups by the dictatorial tyrannies which this nation is now pledged to destroy. To give constitutional sanction to that inference in this case, however well intentioned may have been the military command on the Pacific Coast, is to adopt one of the cruelest of the rationales used by our enemies to destroy the dignity of the individual and to encourage and open the door to discriminatory actions against other minority groups in the passions of tomorrow.

No adequate reason is given for the failure to treat these Japanese Americans on an individual basis by holding investigations and hearings to separate the loyal from the disloyal, as was done in the case of persons of German and Italian ancestry. It is asserted merely that the loyalties of this group "were unknown and time was of the essence." Yet nearly four months elapsed after [Japan attacked] Pearl Harbor before the first exclusion order was issued; nearly eight months went by until the last order was issued, and the last of these "subversive" persons was not actually removed until almost eleven months had elapsed. Leisure and deliberation seem to have been more of the essence than speed. And the fact that conditions were not such as to warrant a declaration of martial law adds strength to the belief that the factors of time and military necessity were not as urgent as they have been represented to be.

An Infringement of Constitutional Rights

Moreover, there was no adequate proof that the Federal Bureau of Investigation and the military and naval intelligence services did not have the espionage and sabotage situation well in hand during this long period. Nor is there any denial of the fact that not one person of Japanese ancestry was accused or convicted of espionage or sabotage after Pearl Harbor while they were still free, a fact which is some evidence of the loyalty of the vast majority of these individuals and of the effectiveness of the established methods of combatting these evils. It seems incredible that, under these circumstances, it would have been impossible to hold loyalty hearings for the mere 112,000 persons involved—or at least for the 70,000 American citizens—especially when a large part of this number represented children and elderly men and women. Any inconvenience that may have accompanied an attempt to conform to procedural due process cannot be said to justify violations of constitutional rights of individuals.

I dissent, therefore, from this legalization of racism. Racial discrimination in any form and in any degree has no justifiable part whatever in our democratic way of life. It is unattractive in any setting but it is utterly revolting among a free people who have embraced the principles set forth in the Constitution of the United States. All residents of this nation are kin in some way by blood or culture to a foreign land. Yet they are primarily and necessarily a part of the new and distinct civilization of the United States. They must, accordingly, be treated at all times as the heirs of the American experiment and as entitled to all the rights and freedoms guaranteed by the Constitution.

> "[The Korematsu decision] planted into American law ... a dangerous precedent for repressive action against minority groups."

Korematsu Set a Dangerous Precedent for Civil Liberties Violations

Morton Grodzing

In the viewpoint that follows, Morton Grodzing alleges that the Supreme Court adopted a surprisingly weak standard of review when it affirmed the conviction of Fred Korematsu, who had violated military orders for all Japanese to evacuate the West Coast during World War II. Grodzing, writing in 1949, accuses the Court of failing to rigorously examine the reasonableness of the military's decree and to consider whether depriving Korematsu and other Japanese Americans of their rights was justified by a "clear and present danger" to the public. In abandoning its usual standards of review in civil liberties cases, the Court made moral and social judgments that may have grave repercussions on civil liberties in the future, Grodzing cautions. Grodzing was a fellow in the political science department at the University of Chicago.

The history of the decision-making process in the evacuation [of Japanese Americans from the West Coast during World War II] is not complete without some clarification of the role of the Supreme Court. Two cases are pertinent, one involving the curfew imposed upon American citizens of Japa-

Morton Grodzing, *Americans Betrayed: Politics and the Japanese Evacuation.* Chicago: University of Chicago Press, 1949. Copyright © 1949 by the University of Chicago. Renewed 1972 by Mrs. Morton Grodzing.

nese ancestry [*Hirabayashi v. United States*]; the other concerned with the evacuation itself [*Korematsu v. United States*]. The Court, hearing both cases long after the events, declared both the curfew and the evacuation constitutional.

The war power of the Congress and the President is, in Justice Charles Hughes's words, "the power to wage war successfully." This is an extensive and flexible power, and the legality of its use can be judged only in the light of an existing situation. The very nature of this power (especially under circumstances of modern warfare demanding military measures far from battle fronts) creates many contingencies which may bring it into conflict with traditional civil liberties.

The Clear-and-Present-Danger Test

Civil liberties are not absolute matters. When liberties come into conflict with pressing public necessities, liberties must give way. Whatever its shortcomings, the famous [Oliver Wendell] Holmes criterion of "clear and present danger" has in recent years been the most frequently utilized test of the United States Supreme Court in determining the legality of civil liberties deprivations: When the larger public stands in "clear and present danger" as the result of the exercise of traditional liberties, then one has no right to those liberties.

But the proximity of danger is not the only factor the Court must consider in civil liberty matters. While it considers constitutional liberties, the Court cannot ignore other constitutional mandates. The government's constitutional power to wage war and the extensive nature of the war power must be balanced against the individual's constitutional rights. The magnitude of the civil liberties deprivation must be judged in terms of the threat to the common welfare.

Under these circumstances the Court may work with a presumption of constitutionality. The clear-and-present-danger test becomes of secondary importance or disappears entirely. The Court simply asks if the administrative or legislative arm of the government can show its action (e.g., the civil liberties deprivation) to be reasonably related to lawful ends (e.g., the waging of war). If such a reasonable relationship can be shown, the Court, using this framework of judicial analysis, will declare the civil liberties violation a constitutional one.

Abandoning Usual Standards of Review

It is this relatively weak standard of review that the Supreme Court utilized in declaring constitutional the curfew and evacuation as applied to American citizens of Japanese ancestry. In considering the circumstances of the curfew, the Court reviewed the nation's perilous military situation in the spring of 1942 and had little difficulty in concluding that "reasonably prudent men charged with responsibility of our national defense had ample ground for concluding that they must face the danger of invasion." Then, examining the evidence brought forward to demonstrate the special danger potential of American citizens of Japanese ancestry, the Court concluded that the curfew was a justifiable war measure. Chief Justice [Harlan] Stone, giving the Court's decision, said:

> Where ... conditions call for the exercise of judgment and discretion and for the choice of means by those branches of the Government on which the Constitution has placed the responsibility of war-making, it is not for any court to sit in review of the wisdom of their action or substitute its judgment for theirs.

> [And later:] ... We cannot reject as unfounded the judgment of the military authorities and of Congress that there were disloyal members of that population, whose number and strength could not be precisely and quickly ascertained. We cannot say the war-making branches of the Government did not have ground for believing ... that prompt and adequate measures [should] be taken. ...

In the same case Mr. Justice [William] Douglas set forth the basis of his concurrence in similarly unmistakable terms:

We must credit the military with as much good faith ... as we would any other public official acting pursuant to his duties.... We cannot sit in judgment on the military requirements of that hour. Where the orders under the present Act have some relation to "protection against espionage and against sabotage," our task is at an end.

Thus, the curfew for Japanese American citizens was declared constitutional because the Court found that it had "some relation" to the winning of the war, because the Court would not "sit in review of the wisdom" of administrative action, because the Court could not say that the government "did not have ground for believing" the curfew was necessary.

The Court Justifies the Mass Evacuation

Exactly the same points were made in the Supreme Court's decision upholding the legality of evacuation itself. Quoting the *Hirabayashi* decision, the Court concluded for exclusion, as for curfew, that "we could not reject the finding of the military authorities that it was impossible to bring about an immediate segregation of the disloyal from the loyal." Evacuation, the Court said in another place, was not "beyond the war power of the Congress and the Executive." Mr. Justice Felix Frankfurter, in a separate concurring opinion, put the point most clearly: "To find that the Constitution does not forbid the military measures now complained of does not carry with it approval of that which Congress and the Executive did. That is their business, not ours."

The language of these decisions demonstrates the care with which the Court made clear its determination to separate acceptance of the legality of evacuation from any hint that it considered evacuation either wise or proper. But the Court's effort in this direction was not made without sacrifice. In its desire to sustain the nation's war-waging powers, the Court sacrificed its usual standards of review in civil liberties cases.

Using a presumption of legality, the Court was able to withdraw itself almost completely from a consideration of evacuation as a civil liberties issue. It needed only to satisfy itself that the evacuation was "reasonably related" to the war effort. If, however, the Court had utilized a more stringent review procedure, the clear-and-present-danger rule, for example, it would inevitably have become involved in a closer and more careful scrutiny of the evacuation.

How completely the Court weakened its review standards has been described brilliantly in an article by Nanette Dembitz. Miss Dembitz has demonstrated that in the crucial *Korematsu* case the Court was exceedingly slack in examining the reasonableness of the evacuation as a necessary war measure. The majority abandoned all tests of clear and present danger, failed to consider whether less drastic measures might not have been reasonably deemed adequate to meet the situation, and accepted without qualification the military reasons brought forward by military officials to support the evacuation policy. The Court's scrutiny of evacuation was significantly less rigorous than its review of the other wartime acts of both civilian and military agencies in conflict with civil liberties. The *Korematsu* majority decision seemed to validate the evacuation largely on the grounds that it was carried out by the War Department. Miss Dembitz has commented that the *Korematsu* opinion "indicates that there is no basis for invalidating war-time actions by military authorities, save perhaps by a showing of malice and a lack of good faith on the part of the military."

Two of the dissenting opinions in the *Korematsu* case were similarly critical of the majority stand. Mr. Justice [Frank] Murphy said that the evacuation fell "into the ugly abyss of racism." Acknowledging the necessity of giving military authorities a wide scope of discretion, he nevertheless asserted that "individuals must not be left impoverished of their constitutional rights on a plea of military necessity that has neither substance nor support." The true test of evacuation, he said, was whether the civil liberties deprivation was "reasonably related to a public danger that is 'so immediate, imminent, and impending' as not to admit of delay and not to permit the intervention of ordinary constitutional processes to alleviate the danger." Mr. Justice Murphy did not find that the evacuation met this test, which is an alternate statement of the clear-and-present-danger rule. He indicated his belief that the Court should have more carefully examined the military reasons which were brought forward to prove the reasonableness of evacuation as a necessary war measure. The Court's opinion, he said, was a "legalization of racism."

Deferrence to Military Judgment

Mr. Justice [Robert] Jackson's dissent attributed the majority's approval of evacuation almost wholly to the fact that evacuation had been ordered by military officials. He argued that "in the very nature of things, military decisions are not susceptible of intelligent judicial appraisal" and that the courts "cannot be made to enforce an order which violates constitutional limitations even if it is a reasonable exercise of military authority." Mr. Justice Jackson condemned court practices that "distort the Constitution to approve all that the military may deem expedient." The Court "may as well say that any military order will be constitutional and have done with it." The type of affirmation of military orders by the Supreme Court, he said, was a "wholly delusive" test of constitutionality.

In approving the evacuation without carefully scrutinizing the issues of civil liberties involved, the Court also gave credence to the doctrines on which the evacuation was based. The Court accepted, in its decisions, much of the half-truth and falsehood that had previously been advanced by West Coast pressure groups and by military leaders in support of evacuation. In the *Hirabayashi* case, for example, the Court noted as evidence supporting the reasonableness of curfew that Japanese Americans were unassimilated; that American citizens of Japanese ancestry attended Japanese-language schools and held dual citizenship; that because "attack on our shores was threatened by Japan rather than another enemy power ... these [American] citizens [of Japanese ancestry were set] apart from others"; that "in time of war residents having ethnic affiliations with an invading enemy may be a greater source of danger than those of a different ancestry." In the *Korematsu* case, to take but one further example, the Court also accepted the military judgment that "it was impossible to bring about an immediate segregation of the loyal from the disloyal." This conclusion was reached despite the fact that the need for "immediate" segregation was not demonstrated and even contradicted by the additional fact that evacuation itself was not completed until five months after its authorization by the President and until eight months after Pearl Harbor. Further, the Court had access to a large amount of information, including the experience of Great Britain in screening German and Austrian aliens, that indicated the feasibility of administering an exclusion program on an individual rather than on a mass basis.

The Court Made Social and Moral Judgments

The separation of legal considerations from public policy considerations is basic to the theory of judicial review. In fact, however, the United States Supreme Court does produce judgments out of the regard of its members for policy issues. In the evacuation cases the Court attempted to withdraw from these issues by the adoption of slack standards of review. But, in a larger sense, the Court by the very process of adopting weak review standards made a social judgment in favor of the evacuation.

It is, therefore, too easy to say that the Court's declaration of the legality of evacuation was no declaration that evacuation was wise or necessary. The more accurate interpretation is paradoxical: Despite its disclaimer, the Court did make a moral and social decision in declaring the evacuation legal. The standard of review utilized did not withdraw the Court from a judgment on the civil liberties issues; rather the review standard simply served to withdraw those issues from the Court's mature consideration.

As simple as the Court's test of evacuation may sound, there is a thin, judicial line separating those restrictive acts that have "some relation" to winning the war from those that do not. The Court was unanimous in upholding the constitutionality of the curfew, but it was divided six to three on the issue of evacuation. Many new facts ... were not before the Court when it heard the evacuation case. If the case could have been heard with the full facts available, it is not unlikely that an adverse decision would have been reached in spite of the wide construction which must be given the war powers.

And this is especially true if the Court adhered to standards of review more compatible with its usual practice in reviewing civil liberties cases. It would have been infinitely more difficult for the Court to have found that evacuation was necessary to meet a "clear and present danger" than it was to find that evacuation was "reasonably related" to winning the war.

Handing Authority a Loaded Weapon

The Court's decision in the curfew and evacuation cases have an importance that cannot yet be fully estimated. In the long run they "expose the constitutional rights of the individual in time of emergency to dangers without precedent," [according to Edward S. Corwin in *Total War and the Constitution*]. In Mr. Justice Jackson's terms, the Court's validation of evacuation remains "like a loaded weapon ready for the hand of any authority that can bring forward a plausible claim of an urgent need."

The decision in the *Korematsu* case, particularly, is difficult to justify. Many factors indicate that the Court should have sharpened, rather than relaxed, its vigilance in considering the constitutionality of evacuation. Notable among these factors were the extreme gravity of the civil liberties deprivation; its racial character; the fact that people were condemned en masse rather than according to the principle of individual liability; and the belief held by many that evacuation was the result of public pressures and racial animosity rather than the result of carefully conceived military policy.

The Court, however, chose the opposite course. Under the circumstances, the Court's decision was a too-easy acquiescence: It planted into American law a dangerous doctrine of military supremacy and a dangerous precedent for repressive action against minority groups.

| *"This hijacking of history is endangering us today."*

Criticism of the Japanese American Evacuation Is Dangerous

Michelle Malkin

A World War II military order to temporarily remove ethnic Japanese from the Pacific Coast was affirmed in Korematsu v. United States. *Michelle Malkin asserts in the following excerpt that the evacuation was necessary in order to protect America from possible attacks assisted by Japanese American spies. Civil libertarians, she points out, often compare the internment of the Japanese to the detainment of Arab Muslims in today's War on Terror, criticizing both as unjust "racial profiling." However, Malkin posits, such preventative practices can thwart acts of war early on and obviate the need for larger infringements on civil liberties later. She suggests that in wartime it is logical to scrutinize Japanese citizens when searching for Japanese spies or to target Arabs when battling Arab Muslim extremists. Besides, Malkin maintains, the 1942 evacuation order had little or no effect on most people of Japanese ancestry. Malkin authored* Invasion, *which discusses immigration and national security in the War on Terror.*

[At the start of World War II,] Mike Masaoka, the national secretary of the Japanese American Citizens League (JACL), the preeminent Japanese American organization, at the time understood and embraced the wartime imperative to put national security first. Explaining why his organization supported the West Coast evacuation of people of Japanese descent and other related military regulations, Masaoka announced in an April 1942 JACL bulletin: "Our primary consideration as good Americans is the total war effort. . . . We may be temporarily suspending or sacrificing some of our privileges and rights of citizenship in the greater aim of protecting them for all time to come and to defeat those powers which seek to destroy them."

Such unequivocal patriotism has been rejected ever since by ethnic activists of all stripes in America (including Masaoka himself, who later in life reversed his position on the evacuation). They are far too busy these days crying racism, demanding apologies, pursuing reparations, suing the government, and obstructing the current war effort in the name of preventing another "Japanese American internment."

Correcting the Record

The phrase "Japanese American internment" belongs in scare quotes because it is historically and legally inaccurate. Hours after the Pearl Harbor attack [by the Japanese], potentially dangerous enemy aliens—not American citizens—from Japan, Germany, and Italy were apprehended, detained, individually screened by review boards composed of prominent citizens, and released, paroled, or sent to internment camps run by the Department of Justice under authority of the Alien Enemies Act of 1798 (which remains in place today). These immediate apprehensions may have played an instrumental role in preventing further havoc on American soil (just as the detention of Middle Eastern illegal aliens following the September 11 attacks [on the United States by Islamic extremists] may have done six decades later). Two months after Pearl Harbor, President [Franklin] Roosevelt signed Executive Order 9066, which led to the mass evacuation and relocation of ethnic Japanese (including both first-generation, permanent resident noncitizen immigrants known as *Issei* and their American-born children known as *Nisei*) from the West Coast.

This latter decision is the one most commonly and erroneously referred to as "internment," "incarceration," or "imprisonment" in America's "concentration camps." In fact, ethnic Japanese living outside of prescribed military zones were not affected by the order. Those who could not or would not leave the West Coast in the spring of 1942 were sent to temporary assembly centers (some of which were later used to house American GIs) and then on to relocation centers run by the War Relocation Authority (WRA) and the Department of Interior. Tens of thousands of evacuees who met national security requirements left the relocation centers for school or work. More than 200 people actually volunteered to enter the camps. When the WRA announced the camps' impending closure in late 1944, many residents protested, demanding that the camps remain open until war's end—or longer.

[*In Defense of Interment: The Case for "Racial Profiling" in World War II and the War on Terror*] challenges the religiously held belief that internment of enemy aliens and the West Coast evacuation and relocation of ethnic Japanese were primarily the result of "wartime hysteria" and "race prejudice." That was the conclusion of a national panel, the Commission on Wartime Relocation and Internment of Civilians, in 1981, which stated, "We firmly believe that it should be common knowledge that the detention of Americans of Japanese ancestry during World War II was not an act of military necessity but an act of racial discrimination." This finding was the basis for a federal reparations bill granting nearly $2 billion to ethnic Japanese evacuees and internees. And it is the premise of virtually every high school and college history lesson on national security measures taken during World War II.

Leading critics of the World War II evacuation and relocation don't just argue that the military rationale for Roosevelt's actions was insufficient. They make the extremely radical and historically dishonest argument that there was no military justification whatsoever for evacuation, relocation, or internment—and that America's top political and military leaders knew this at the time. Roosevelt's decisions, according to this conventional view, were adopted to mollify West Coast politicians who were pandering to racism, hysteria, and economic opportunism among their nativist constituents. According to the JACL curriculum guide used by public school teachers nationwide, the West Coast evacuation was the result not of a sincere desire to protect the West Coast but of "prejudice," "legal discrimination," and the "culmination of the movement to eliminate Asians . . . that began nearly 100 years earlier." In arguing for a congressional resolution in March 2004 to establish a "National Day of Remembrance for the restriction, exclusion and internment of individuals and families during World War II," Representative Mike Honda (a Democrat from California), an evacuee who had resided in the Granada, Colorado, relocation center as a child, asserted that the West Coast evacuation "was based on neither reason nor evidence but on fear and panic." This version of history has been perpetuated by hundreds of books, videos, plays, and websites, many of them subsidized with public funds.

A Warped Yardstick

Why write [*In Defense of Internment*] now? Because the prevailing view of World War II homeland defense measures has become the warped yardstick by which all War on Terror measures today are judged. In truth, the U.S. government's national security concerns during World War II, particularly the threat of espionage in support of the Japanese emperor, were real and urgent.

When former Attorney General Janet Reno declared in 2003 that there was absolutely "no record" that any Japanese Americans posed a security threat during World War II, she demonstrated a common, utter ignorance of the matter. American intelligence teams had decoded top-secret Japanese diplomatic cables, dubbed MAGIC, revealing an aggressive effort to recruit West Coast spies, including both Japanese aliens (*Issei*) and U.S.-born citizens of Japanese descent (*Nisei*). Just as the VENONA decrypts of Soviet diplomatic communications revealed the long-hidden truth about Russia's extensive espionage attempts to infiltrate the United States during the Cold War, the MAGIC decrypts exposed in startling detail how Japan had succeeded in establishing a formidable West Coast espionage network by mid-1941. After Pearl Harbor, U.S. intelligence agencies believed that this network remained in place. With Pearl Harbor in ruins and the Japanese Navy in nearly complete control of the Pacific—its submarines looming off our coastline—it would have been irresponsible to dismiss the possibility of attacks on the mainland assisted by West Coast fifth columnists of Japanese ancestry.

In the face of rabid ethnic activism, historical revisionism, and political capitulation, few have defended the wartime measures undertaken to protect the West Coast—or even acknowledged that the decision to implement them was a close call. The national security concerns so clearly delineated in the intelligence memos of the time are ignored. The War Department officials who pored over MAGIC messages every night are said to have had only crass political motives. Even the venerable U.S. Supreme Court Justice William Rehnquist, who provides a partial defense of the West Coast evacuation in *All the Laws But One*, gives only a superficial treatment of the role of intelligence in Roosevelt's decision-making. As the late David Lowman, a former National Security Agency official who participated in the declassification of MAGIC and wrote a groundbreaking book on the subject, noted, "Seldom has any major event in U.S. history been as misrepresented as has U.S. intelligence related to the evacuation. It has been twisted, distorted, misquoted, misunderstood, ignored, and deliberately falsified by otherwise honorable people. . . . The United States did not act shamefully, dishonorably, and without reason as charged."

Roosevelt's defenders have been (and will continue to be) vilified and viciously smeared as morally equivalent to Holocaust deniers. Consider the reaction to Representative Howard Coble (a Republican from North Carolina) in February 2003 after he asserted that the West Coast evacuation and relocation was justified. "For many of these Japanese Americans, it wasn't safe for them to be on the street," Coble said. "Some probably were intent on doing harm to us, just as some of these Arab-Americans are probably intent on doing harm to us." Coble, who serves as chairman of the House Judiciary Committee on Crime, Terrorism and Homeland Security, made clear that he did not support such drastic measures in the current War on Terror, but argued that Roosevelt's decision was justified in its time. His remarks prompted protests by the [civil rights groups] AFL-CIO, the NAACP, and the Democratic National Committee chairman [Terry McAuliffe], who said Coble was "not fit to lead our country on security and constitutional matters and must resign from the chairmanship." JACL also called for Coble's head, ignoring the fact that its own leaders made some of the same arguments in support of evacuation and relocation during the war. It is "a sad day in our country's tradition when an elected official . . . openly agrees with an unconstitutional [sic] and racist policy," the American-Arab Anti-Discrimination Committee huffed. The California State Assembly condemned Coble; Hawaii legislators called on the House Judiciary committee to "educate and sensitize" members about Japanese Americans during World War II. Coble kept his job, but was forced to apologize, "We all know now that this was in fact the wrong decision and an action that should never be repeated."

A Return to *Korematsu*?

U.S. Civil Rights Commissioner Peter Kirsanow received similar treatment from Japanese American and Arab American activists in the summer of 2002. During a panel hearing on racial profiling in Detroit, Noel John Saleh, an attorney and a member of the Detroit chapter of the American-Arab Anti-Discrimination Committee, stated, "[The current situation] does lead and could well lead to situations as embarrassing as the Japanese internment camps in the Second World War . . . if there is in fact another terrorist attack on the United States, then such things can be revisited." Commissioner Kirsanow, a conservative Bush appointee, responded "that homeland security may be one of the best ways of protecting civil rights because as you alluded to, I believe no matter how many laws we have, how many agencies we have, how many police officers we have monitoring civil rights, that if there's another terrorist attack and if it's from a certain ethnic community or certain ethnicities that the terrorists are from, you can forget civil rights in this country. I think we will have a return to *Korematsu* [the 1944 Supreme Court decision that affirmed the constitutionality of the West Coast exclusion orders during World War II] and I think the best way we can thwart that is to make sure that there is a balance between protecting civil rights, but also protecting safety at the same time."

Kirsanow wasn't endorsing a roundup of Arab Muslims. He was merely observing that adopting lesser measures that the ethnic grievance industry vehemently protests as civil rights atrocities—such things as airport profiling, targeted illegal alien sweeps, monitoring of mosques, and tighter visa screening procedures—can prevent acts of terrorism, which in turn can prevent larger infringements on civil liberties down the road. Some may disagree with Kirsanow's assertion, but it is hardly a radical view. Nevertheless, the "Japanese American internment" has become such a sacred cow that even the mildest of considered comments related to it invites blind and vicious retribution. An apoplectic team of Japanese American lawyers who had worked unsuccessfully to get the Supreme Court to overturn *Korematsu* demanded that the Bush administration fire him [Kirsanow]. They railed that Kirsanow's "inflammatory rhetoric ... now threatens to victimize innocent Arab Americans." Lawyer Dale Minami added, "What he has done is raise the level of hysteria in this country." Devon Alisa Abdallah penned an opinion piece headlined "Arab Community Pack Your Bags: Civil Rights Commissioner doesn't believe in civil rights." The Leadership Conference on Civil Rights wrote that Kirsanow's remarks were "shocking, irresponsible, outrageous, and should be unacceptable." Imad Hamad of the American-Arab Anti-Discrimination Committee fumed, "For someone in [Kirsanow's] position to even entertain the idea of detention camps, it is like he is making it an acceptable debate."

Even those who simply profess lack of knowledge about the topic are subjected to scathing criticism. When Middle East scholar Daniel Pipes, whom the Bush administration nominated to serve on the U.S. Institute of Peace, stated in an interview that he didn't know enough about the World War II evacuation and relocation of ethnic Japanese to comment on whether he supported it, ethnic activists launched an immediate attack. "Bush nominee refuses to condemn Japanese internment," the Council on American-Islamic Relations (CAIR) proclaimed. "It is outrageous that someone with undergraduate and doctoral degrees from Harvard University, both in history, would fail to condemn the unjust internment of Japanese Americans by disingenuously claiming he is ill-informed," CAIR executive director Nihad Awad bellowed.

The real outrage lies in the smug orthodoxy of the civil liberties absolutists, to whom intellectual honesty poses a dire threat. The politically correct myth of American "concentration camps" has become enshrined as incontrovertible wisdom in the gullible press, postmodern academia, the cash-hungry grievance industry, and liberal Hollywood. This hijacking of history is endangering us today.

Connecting the Dots

Civil liberties absolutists have invoked the World War II evacuation and relocation of ethnic Japanese to attack virtually every homeland security initiative aimed at protecting America from murderous Islamic extremists. Within weeks of the September 11 attacks, Japanese American activists rushed to comfort Arab and Muslim Americans who felt unfairly targeted. "War on Terrorism Stirs Memory of Internment," the *New York Times* decried. "Japanese Americans Recall 40s Bias, Understand Arab Counterparts' Fear," read a *Washington Post* headline. "Japanese Americans Know How It Feels to Be 'The Enemy,'" the *Seattle Times* reported. "Reaction Reopens Wound of WWII for Japanese Americans," the *Los Angeles Times* noted.

Irene Hirano, executive director and president of the Japanese American National Museum, lamented, "Now, as in 1942 when America came under attack, the resulting emotions are: anger, hate, vengeance, and patriotism." The National Asian Pacific American Legal Consortium (NAPALC) said that "solidarity between communities identified as 'the enemy' has in some cases forged a new alliance between Japanese Americans and Arab Americans and Muslims." NAPALC President Karen Narasaki proclaimed: "No one should be presumed to be any less loyal to our country just because of the color of their skin, their national origin, their immigration status or the religion that they follow."

Soon after September 11, the Justice Department began interviewing Arab and Muslim foreigners for investigative leads. Although participation was strictly voluntary, commentator Julianne Malveaux complained, "It's beginning to look like the Japanese internment." When two men were removed from a Continental Airlines flight in December 2001 based on the plane crew's security concerns, the ejected passengers (a Guyanese American and a Filipino immigrant) promptly filed racial discrimination lawsuits. Their American Civil Liberties Union lawyer, Reginald Shuford, didn't miss a beat: "The Japanese internment issue is the model for this type of thing. We look back in embarrassment upon that period in our history, as we will upon this." When Attorney General John Ashcroft so much as sneezed, he triggered flashbacks of "internment" and howls of protest about "racial profiling"—including from a fellow cabinet member of the Bush administration.

Stubborn Backlash Against Racial Profiling

Department of Transportation Secretary Norm Mineta, who was evacuated as a young boy from San Jose, California, to a relocation center in Heart Mountain, Wyoming, declared that any profiling taking into account race, ethnicity, religion, or nationality would be forbidden in airport security. He complained, "I think we are seeing shades of what we experienced in 1942." When asked by CBS's *60 Minutes* correspondent Steve Croft whether he could envision any circumstance where it would make sense to use racial and ethnic profiling, Mineta responded, "Absolutely not." Croft persisted, "Are you saying at the security screening desks, that a 70-year-old white woman from Vero Beach, Florida, would receive the same level of scrutiny as a Muslim young man from Jersey City?" Mineta replied, "Basically, I would hope so." Croft followed up, "If you saw three young Arab men sitting, kneeling, praying, before they boarded a flight, getting on, talking to each other in Arabic, getting on the plane, no reason to stop and ask them any questions? "No reason," Mineta stubbornly declared.

And what if he had seen the names Khalid Al-Midhar, Majed Moqed, Nawaf Alhamzi, Salem Alhamzi, and Hani Hanjour on a passenger manifest? Or Satam Al Suqami, Waleed M. Alshehri, Mohammed Atta, Wail Alsheri, and Abdulaziz Alomari? Or Marwan Al-Shehhi, Fayez Ahmed, Ahmed Alghamdi, Hamza Alghamdi, and Mohald Alshehri? Or Saeed Alghamdi, Ahmed Alhaznawi, Ahmed Alnami, and Ziad Jarrah? What if those four groups of September 11 hijackers were resurrected from hell and attempted to board airplanes today? Would their observable characteristics—young men of

Arab appearance with Arab-sounding names and Arabic accents—be reason enough to search them and their luggage, perhaps revealing clues, such as box cutters or Mohammed Atta's suicide note, that would have set off alarm bells? In Mineta's mind, so fixed on his childhood past as to blind him to the present threats to our nation, absolutely not.

> "Korematsu . . . *stands a constant cau-*
> *tion that in times of war . . . our institu-*
> *tions must be vigilant in protecting con-*
> *stitutional guarantees."*

The Overturning of *Korematsu* Affirmed Civil Liberties

Dale Ikeda

Superior Court judge Dale Ikeda argues in the following selection that justice was finally achieved in the 1980s when a judge vacated the 1944 conviction of Fred Korematsu. During World War II Korematsu had remained on the West Coast after the military ordered all members of the Japanese race to leave the area. Korematsu and other Japanese Americans were then placed in relocation camps. Ikeda avows that this treatment violated the constitutional rights of Japanese Americans. The eventual overturning of Korematsu *and two other cases, along with the government's apology and the payments it offered to surviving internees, reaffirmed the core American values of equality and fairness, contends Ikeda.*

It is truly an honor for me to tell the story of Japanese Americans interned during World War II and their successful campaign for Redress. ("Redress" is a concept rooted in the First Amendment of the U.S. Constitution. It is the right of the people to petition the government for redress of grievances.) The story starts with the policy of exclusion and the forced removal of more than 120,000 Americans of Japanese ancestry, mostly citizens, from the West Coast. It ends with the enactment and implementation of the Civil Liberties

Dale Ikeda, "The Japanese American Story of Internment and Redress," Fresno County Bar Association, April 7, 2004. Copyright © 2004 by Dale Ikeda. Reproduced by permission.

Act of 1988 ("Act" or "Redress Legislation"). The House of Representatives passed the Act, on the 200th Anniversary of the signing of the Constitution. . . .

Military Orders Based on Racism

On March 2, 1942, General [John D.] DeWitt established "Military Area No. 1," which included the western parts of California, Oregon and Washington and the southern part of Arizona.

Beginning on March 24, 1942, General DeWitt issued a series of orders applying to persons of Japanese ancestry residing in Military Area No. 1. These orders included the establishment of a curfew for Japanese Americans between the hours of 8:00 P.M. and 6:00 A.M.; a requirement that such persons report to "assembly centers"; and, a requirement that such persons leave designated areas in the military area to "relocation centers" established further inland. The concentration camps in which Japanese Americans were imprisoned were located in desolate and isolated places such as Manzanar and Tule Lake in California; Minidoka in Idaho; Topaz in Utah; Poston and Gila in Arizona; Heart Mountain in Wyoming; Grenada in Colorado; and Jerome and Rohwer in Arkansas. The internees lived behind barbwire fences under military control. Guard towers with soldiers armed with rifles and machine guns were located around the perimeter of the camps.

General DeWitt justified the exclusion of Japanese Americans from the West Coast on the grounds that there was no way to distinguish the loyal from the disloyal. DeWitt believed that the racial characteristics of Japanese Americans predisposed them to disloyalty. DeWitt appeared before a Congressional committee (Select Committee Investigating National Defense Migration of the House of Representatives, chaired by John H. Tolan, also known as the "Tolan Committee") to testify: "A Jap's a Jap. They are a dangerous element. . . . There is no way to determine their loyalty. . . . It makes no difference whether he is an American citizen; theoretically he is still a Japanese and you can't change him. . . . " He wrote in his final report, "In the war in which we are now engaged racial affinities are not severed by migration. The Japanese race is an enemy race and while many second and third generation Japanese born on United States soil, possessed of United States citizenship, have become 'Americanized,' the racial strains are undiluted." (During the five months between the attack on Pearl Harbor and removal, there were no acts of sabotage or espionage by Japanese Americans.)

Conditions of the "Relocation Centers"

The Japanese Americans were removed from the West Coast and held in so-called "relocation centers" for almost three years during the War. . . . The Notice of Civilian Exclusion Order No. 33 issued by General DeWitt dated May 3, 1942 instructs persons of Japanese ancestry, both alien and "non-alien" (citizens) to report to assembly centers within two days. They were only allowed to take what they could carry. Locally, assembly centers were established at the Fresno Fairgrounds and in Pinedale [California]. For reasons beyond comprehension, residents of Washington and Oregon were brought to Pinedale from their cool climate to suffer in the heat of Fresno's summer without air conditioning. Several people died.

Perhaps it would give some context if I mentioned my family's history. My dad and uncle grew up north of Clovis [California] and graduated from Clovis High School. My grandfather was the foreman at Alta Sierra Ranch, now site of Buchanan High School and residential subdivisions. Prior to the attack on Pearl Harbor, my uncle joined the U.S. Army. My Dad met my Mom, who graduated from Edison High School in Fresno. Her family lived on "F" Street near Ventura. My dad had to violate curfew and travel restrictions in order to see her. They married before being relocated so that they could stay together. My father's family voluntarily joined my mother's family at the Fresno Assembly Center, even though they had not yet been ordered to do so by the military authorities. They were there from May through October 1942, before being relocated to Jerome, Arkansas, where my oldest brother, George, was born. My dad mentioned how difficult it was for couples to have any privacy. They lived in a barrack with other families without walls. They hung sheets to create some semi-private areas. . . .

Three Dissenting Justices in the *Korematsu* Case

[The military's order to evacuate was upheld in] the case of Fred Korematsu. Mr. Korematsu remained in San Leandro, California, to be with his Caucasian girlfriend. He was convicted of violating General DeWitt's Civilian Exclusion Order No. 34. In a 6-to-3 decision, the U.S. Supreme Court affirmed the lower courts and upheld the conviction of Mr. Korematsu, again deferring to the military's judgment. Such deference is in stark contrast to current court standards, which impose "strict judicial scrutiny" of governmental action resulting in invidious discrimination based on race or national origin. Today, governmental action must further a "compelling state interest" utilizing the "least restrictive means" available in order to satisfy equal protection and due process standards.

Justices William O. Douglas and Felix Frankfurter sided with the majority. If these reputed civil libertarians had sided with Justices [Robert] Jackson, [Owen] Roberts and [Frank] Murphy, the exclusion orders would have been stricken down as a violation of the constitutional guarantees of due process and equal protection.

Justice [Hugo] Black for the majority stated:

Like curfew, exclusion of those of Japanese origin was deemed necessary because of the presence of an unascertained number of disloyal members of the group, most of

81

whom we have no doubt were loyal to this country. It was *because we could not reject the finding of the military authority that it was impossible to bring about an immediate segregation of the disloyal and the loyal* that we sustained the validity of the curfew order as applying to the whole group. In the instant case, temporary exclusion of the entire group was rested by the military on the same ground. The judgment that *exclusion of the whole group was* for the same reason *a military imperative* answers the contention that the exclusion was in the nature of group punishment based on antagonism to those of Japanese origin. [Emphasis added.]

Justices Murphy, Roberts and Jackson filed separate dissenting opinions. Justice Murphy stated:

Being an obvious racial discrimination, the [exclusion] order deprives all those within its scope of the equal protection of the laws as guaranteed by the Fifth Amendment. . . . In excommunicating them without benefit of hearings, this order also deprives them of all their constitutional rights to procedural due process. Yet no reasonable relation to an "immediate, imminent, and impending" public danger is evident to support this racial restriction which is one of the most sweeping and complete deprivations of constitutional rights to procedural due process in the history of this nation in the absence of martial law.

. . . .

Nor is there any denial of the fact that *not one person of Japanese ancestry was accused or convicted of espionage or sabotage after Pearl Harbor while they were still free, a fact which is some evidence of the loyalty of the vast majority of these individuals* and of the effectiveness of the established methods of combatting these evils.

. . . .

I dissent, therefore, from this legalization of racism. Racial discrimination in any form and in any degree has no justifiable part whatever in our democratic way of life. It is unattractive in any setting but it *is utterly revolting among a free people who have embraced the principles set forth in the Constitution of the United States.* [Emphasis added.]

Justice Jackson, who later became the chief prosecutor in the *Nuremberg* trials, stated: "If any fundamental assumption underlies our system, it is that guilt is personal and not inheritable." He went on to observe that:

> Once a judicial opinion rationalizes such an order or rather rationalized the Constitution to show that the Constitution sanctions such an order, *the Court for all time has validated the principle of racial discrimination in criminal procedure and of transplanting American citizens.* The principle then lies about like a *loaded weapon* ready for the hand of an authority that can bring forward a plausible claim for an urgent need. Every repetition imbeds that principle more deeply in our law and thinking and expands it to new purposes. [Emphasis added.] ...

Fighting for Justice

The righteousness of the Redress effort was hampered by the U.S. Supreme Court's decisions in the *Korematsu, Hirabayashi* and *Yasui* cases.[1]

However, a dedicated team of attorneys fought to have the criminal convictions of Min Yasui, Gordon Hirabayashi and Fred Korematsu vacated. In the 1980s, they succeeded through an extraordinary writ of error *coram nobis*. (It is a common law writ to invalidate a criminal conviction after the sentence has been served to prevent manifest injustice.)

The team was led by [political science professor] Peter Irons. I spoke to Dr. Irons on April 29th. He described a fateful meeting he had with Aiko Herzig-Yoshinaga and her husband Jack Herzig. He was conducting archival research for a book he was writing on the *Korematsu* case. The documents

---

1. In *Hirabayashi* and *Yasui*, the Court upheld a curfew applied only to people of Japanese ancestry.

he was looking for had been checked out by the Herzigs. Aiko was the chief researcher for the Commission on Wartime Relocation and Internment of Civilians. Aiko had located the original version of General DeWitt's Final Report on the exclusion and detention orders sitting on the desk of an archivist at the National Archives in 1982. The Report stated: "It was impossible to establish the identity of the loyal and disloyal. *It was not there was insufficient time in which to make such a determination: it was simply a matter of facing the realities that a positive determination could not be made, that an exact separation of the "sheep from the goats" was unfeasible.*" The War Department submitted an altered final report to the courts to eliminate contradictions in the representations already made to the courts that there was *no time* to separate the loyal from the disloyal. The altered version states: "To complicate the situation, *no ready means existed for determining the loyal from the disloyal* with any degree of safety. It was necessary to face the realities—a positive determination could not be made." Both DeWitt's assertion and the War Department's position were contradicted by the Federal Bureau of Investigation and other governmental agencies, but that information was ignored by DeWitt, the War Department and the Department of Justice and never presented to the courts. The War Department systematically sought to destroy all copies of the original report. The copy located by Mrs. Herzig is the only known copy which escaped destruction.

In a letter that Mr. Irons wrote to Fred Korematsu, he explained the nature of the petition and its basis. He explained, "what this means in English (lawyers like to use Latin to make people think what they do is mysterious) is that you would be asking the original trial court (in your case, the federal court in San Francisco) to correct a fundamental error and injustice at your trial. The error would be the failure of the government to acknowledge that there was no evidence to support General DeWitt's claim that acts of sabotage and espionage by Japanese Americans required the curfew and evacuation, and no evidence to support his claim that Japanese Americans were disloyal. We now know, in fact, from government documents that General DeWitt had been told that there was no such evidence before he issued the curfew and evacuation orders, and that he disregarded what he had been told. Since the government had this evidence at the time of your trial, it was under an obligation to produce it. By failing to produce it, the court's judgment of guilty in your case was based on error and a fundamental injustice was committed. Since the government also failed to correct this error when the case was appealed to the Court of Appeals and then to the Supreme Court, the final decision in your case was also fundamentally unjust." . . .

A Victory for Civil Rights

The petitions were filed January 19, 1983, a month after the Commission on Wartime Relocation and Internment of Civilians ("Commission") issued its findings that Executive Order No. 9066 was not justified by military necessity. The legal team was overjoyed when Fred Korematsu's petition was assigned to Judge Marilyn Patel. ([Attorney] Dale Minami told me recently how Judge Patel was their first choice of judges to hear the case.) . . .

In Judge Patel's decision, she noted that the government deliberately omitted relevant information and provided misleading information in papers before the court. She went on to state:

> In *Korematsu v. United States* . . . the judicial process is seriously impaired when the government's law enforcement officers violate their ethical obligations to the court.
>
> *Korematsu* remains on the pages of our legal and political history. As a legal precedent it is now recognized as having very limited application. As historical precedent, it *stands a constant caution that in times of war or declared military ne-*

cessity our institutions must be vigilant in protecting constitutional guarantees. It stands as a caution that in times of distress the shield of military necessity and national security must not be used to protect governmental actions from close scrutiny and accountability. It stands as a caution that in times of international hostility and antagonisms our institutions, legislative, executive and judicial, must be prepared to exercise their authority to protect all citizens from the petty fears and prejudices that are so easily aroused. [Emphasis added.] . . .

Recommendations of the Commission

The findings and conclusions of the Commission were unanimous. The Commission concluded that at the time of issuance of Executive Order No. 9066 and implementing military orders, there was substantial credible evidence from a number of federal civilians and military agencies contradicting the report of General DeWitt that military necessity justified exclusions and internment of all persons of Japanese ancestry without regard to individual identification of those who may have been potentially disloyal.

The Commission found that *military necessity did not warrant the exclusion and detention of Japanese Americans*. It concluded that "broad historical causes which shaped these decisions were race prejudice, war hysteria and a failure of political leadership." As a result, "a *grave injustice* was done to American citizens and resident aliens of Japanese ancestry who, without individual review or any probative evidence against them, were excluded, removed and detained by the United States during World War II," [according to the Commission's report,] *Personal Justice Denied*. The Commission recommended monetary compensation of $20,000.00 as a symbolic payment to redress the government's actions.

CHAPTER 3

Striking Down
Prior Restraint

Case Overview

New York Times Co. v. United States (1971)

In 1971, while the United States was fighting the Vietnam War, many Americans felt deep dismay that their country had not quickly defeated North Vietnam as had been expected. As the fighting dragged on, former Pentagon analyst Daniel Ellsberg leaked to the *New York Times* thousands of pages of a classified report pertaining to the war. As the *Times* pored over the report, it discovered surprising disclosures, including the government's true aims in Vietnam, its pessimism about winning the war, and its deception regarding air strikes and boat attacks. The *Times* began to print the documents, which came to be known as the Pentagon Papers, in regular installments. The press, it seemed, had departed from its typically trusting attitude toward government officials and had begun to question the president's decisions and foreign policy. Correspondent Don Oberdorfer notes that when the report was printed newspapers finally "became independent of the government on the war."

As important as the Pentagon Papers were, the public did not take immediate notice. But Attorney General John Mitchell did. He ordered the *Times* to stop printing the stolen documents and to return them to the government. Countering that prior restraint—the practice of censoring a story before it is printed—is prohibited by the First Amendment, the newspaper refused. In response the government sought a temporary restraining order to prevent the paper from publishing more of the report. Mitchell and other officials asserted that because the country was still involved in the war, printing the sensitive documents could do "irreparable injury" to the United States. Therefore, they maintained, the use of censorship was justified. The court granted the temporary restraint. This was a historic act, as Supreme Court justice William Brennan later noted: "Never before has the United States sought to enjoin a newspaper from publishing information in its possession."

Soon the *Times* case landed in federal district court, where Judge Murray Gurfein determined that the government had produced no evidence of its claim that the document's release would cause irreparable harm. Accordingly, he denied a permanent injunction against the *Times*. Due to the time-sensitive nature of newspaper publishing, the *Times* appeal reached the Supreme Court fifteen days after litigation began. By this time the *Washington Post* had begun publishing its own summary of the Pentagon Papers, and the government had sought an injunction against it as well. Because of their similarities *New York Times Co. v. United States* and *United States v. Washington Post Co.* were decided together.

The Court splintered in the decision, producing six separate opinions and three dissents. In his dissent Chief Justice Warren Burger called for limitations on the rights of the press:

> The newspapers make a derivative claim under the First Amendment; they denominate this right as the public "right to know." . . . The right is asserted as an absolute. Of course, the First Amendment right itself is not an absolute, as Justice [Oliver Wendell] Holmes so long ago pointed out in his aphorism concerning the right to shout 'fire' in a crowded theater if there was no fire.

Ultimately the Court ruled that the government had not met its heavy burden of showing that prior restraint was justified. Thus, the Pentagon Papers decision implies that even in wartime, the press has rights that cannot be abridged. As Justice William Douglas opined, "The First Amendment provides that 'Congress shall make no law abridging the freedom of speech, or of the press.' That leaves, in my view, no room for governmental restraint on the press."

> "Only a free and unrestrained press can effectively expose deception in government."

The Court's Decision: Reinforcing the Rights of the Press

Hugo Black

In New York Times Co. v. United States, *the Supreme Court examined the legality of a restraining order that prevented a newspaper from publishing classified reports of U.S. involvement in the Vietnam War. In Justice Hugo Black's concurring opinion, from which the following viewpoint is excerpted, he argues that the order breaches the First Amendment right to a free press. The Constitution explicitly protects this right, he asserts, because an unrestrained press is necessary in order to preserve democracy and prevent the government from deceiving its citizens. To curtail this right, Black notes, would be to completely and disastrously alter a constitutional right that the founding fathers labeled as "inviolable." Moreover, he points out, neither the Court nor the president has the power to make a law abridging press freedom. Black was nominated to the Supreme Court in 1937 and served until 1971.*

I adhere to the view that the Government's case against the *Washington Post* should have been dismissed and that the injunction against the *New York Times* should have been vacated without oral argument when the cases were first presented to this Court. I believe that every moment's continuance of the injunctions against these newspapers amounts to a flagrant, indefensible, and continuing violation of the First

Hugo Black, concurring opinion, *New York Times Co. v. United States,* 403 U.S. 713, June 30, 1971.

Amendment. Furthermore, after oral argument, I agree completely that we must affirm the judgment of the Court of Appeals for the District of Columbia Circuit and reverse the judgment of the Court of Appeals for the Second Circuit for the reasons stated by my Brothers [William] Douglas and [William] Brennan. In my view it is unfortunate that some of my Brethren are apparently willing to hold that the publication of news may sometimes be enjoined. Such a holding would make a shambles of the First Amendment.

Our Government was launched in 1789 with the adoption of the Constitution. The Bill of Rights, including the First Amendment, followed in 1791. Now, for the first time in the 182 years since the founding of the Republic, the federal courts are asked to hold that the First Amendment does not mean what it says, but rather means that the Government can halt the publication of current news of vital importance to the people of this country.

First Amendment Protections

In seeking injunctions against these newspapers and in its presentation to the Court, the Executive Branch seems to have forgotten the essential purpose and history of the First Amendment. When the Constitution was adopted, many people strongly opposed it because the document contained no Bill of Rights to safeguard certain basic freedoms. They especially feared that the new powers granted to a central government might be interpreted to permit the government to curtail freedom of religion, press, assembly, and speech. In response to an overwhelming public clamor, James Madison offered a series of amendments to satisfy citizens that these great liberties would remain safe and beyond the power of government to abridge. Madison proposed what later became the First Amendment in three parts, two of which are set out below, and one of which proclaimed: "The people shall not be deprived or abridged of their right to speak, to write, or to publish their sentiments; and the freedom of the press, as one of the great bulwarks of liberty, shall be inviolable." The amendments were offered to curtail and restrict the general powers granted to the Executive, Legislative, and Judicial Branches two years before in the original Constitution. The Bill of Rights changed the original Constitution into a new charter under which no branch of government could abridge the people's freedoms of press, speech, religion, and assembly. Yet the Solicitor General argues and some members of the Court appear to agree that the general powers of the Government adopted in the original Constitution should be interpreted to limit and restrict the specific and emphatic guarantees of the Bill of Rights adopted later. I can imagine no greater perversion of history. Madison and the other Framers of the First Amendment, able men that they were, wrote in language they earnestly believed could never be misunderstood: "Congress shall make no law . . . abridging the freedom . . . of the press. . . ." Both the history and language of the First Amendment support the view that the press must be left free to publish news, whatever the source, without censorship, injunctions, or prior restraints.

In the First Amendment the Founding Fathers gave the free press the protection it must have to fulfill its essential role in our democracy. The press was to serve the governed, not the governors. The Government's power to censor the press was abolished so that the press would remain forever free to censure the Government. The press was protected so that it could bare the secrets of government and inform the people. Only a free and unrestrained press can effectively expose deception in government. And paramount among the responsibilities of a free press is the duty to prevent any part of the government from deceiving the people and sending them off to distant lands to die of foreign fevers and foreign shot and shell. In my view, far from deserving condemnation for their courageous reporting, the *New York Times,* the *Washington*

Post, and other newspapers should be commended for serving the purpose that the Founding Fathers saw so clearly. In revealing the workings of government that led to the Vietnam war, the newspapers nobly did precisely that which the Founders hoped and trusted they would do.

The Press and National Security

The Government's case here is based on premises entirely different from those that guided the Framers of the First Amendment. The Solicitor General has carefully and emphatically stated:

> Now, Mr. Justice [Black], your construction of . . . [the First Amendment] is well known, and I certainly respect it. You say that no law means no law, and that should be obvious. I can only say, Mr. Justice, that to me it is equally obvious that 'no law' does not mean 'no law', and I would seek to persuade the Court that is true. . . . There are other parts of the Constitution that grant powers and responsibilities to the Executive, and . . . the First Amendment was not intended to make it impossible for the Executive to function or to protect the security of the United States.

And the Government argues in its brief that in spite of the First Amendment, "[t]he authority of the Executive Department to protect the nation against publication of information whose disclosure would endanger the national security stems from two interrelated sources: the constitutional power of the President over the conduct of foreign affairs and his authority as Commander-in-Chief."

In other words, we are asked to hold that despite the First Amendment's emphatic command, the Executive Branch, the Congress, and the Judiciary can make laws enjoining publication of current news and abridging freedom of the press in the name of "national security." The Government does not even attempt to rely on any act of Congress. Instead it makes the bold and dangerously far-reaching contention that the courts should take it upon themselves to "make" a law abridging freedom of the press in the name of equity, presidential power and national security, even when the representatives of the people in Congress have adhered to the command of the First Amendment and refused to make such a law. To find that the President has "inherent power" to halt the publication of news by resort to the courts would wipe out the First Amendment and destroy the fundamental liberty and security of the very people the Government hopes to make "secure." No one can read the history of the adoption of the First Amendment without being convinced beyond any doubt that it was injunctions like those sought here that Madison and his collaborators intended to outlaw in this Nation for all time.

Security Lies in Constitutional Rights

The word "security" is a broad, vague generality whose contours should not be invoked to abrogate the fundamental law embodied in the First Amendment. The guarding of military and diplomatic secrets at the expense of informed representative government provides no real security for our Republic. The Framers of the First Amendment, fully aware of both the need to defend a new nation and the abuses of the English and Colonial governments, sought to give this new society strength and security by providing that freedom of speech, press, religion, and assembly should not be abridged. This thought was eloquently expressed in 1937 by Mr. Chief Justice [Charles] Hughes—great man and great Chief Justice that he was—when the Court held a man could not be punished for attending a meeting run by Communists.

> The greater the importance of safeguarding the community from incitements to the overthrow of our institutions by force and violence, the more imperative is the need to preserve inviolate the constitutional rights of free speech, free press and free assembly in order to maintain the opportu-

nity for free political discussion, to the end that government may be responsive to the will of the people and that changes, if desired, may be obtained by peaceful means. Therein lies the security of the Republic, the very foundation of constitutional government.

> *"I cannot subscribe to a doctrine of un-*
> *limited absolutism for the First Amend-*
> *ment at the cost of downgrading other*
> *provisions."*

Dissenting Opinion: Demanding Press Responsibility

Harry Blackmun

When the government sought an injunction to prevent a news-
paper from printing a classified report during the Vietnam War,
it was denied. Justice Harry Blackmun, in his following dissent
in New York Times Co. v. United States, *maintains that the re-*
straint should have been granted because the press had neglected
its duty to not harm the interests of the United States. The sen-
sitive nature of the documents, Blackmun believes, could cause
soldiers to die, alliances to fail, or negotiations to break down. If
these outcomes should now occur, he warns, the press alone bears
the responsibility, for press freedom should never come at the ex-
pense of national security. Blackmun served on the Court from
1970 to 1994.

At this point the focus is on only the comparatively few documents specified by the Government as critical. So far as the other material—vast in amount—is concerned, let it be published and published forthwith if the newspapers, once the strain is gone and the sensationalism is eased, still feel the urge so to do.

But we are concerned here with the few documents specified from the 47 volumes. Almost 70 years ago Mr. Justice

Harry Blackmun, dissenting opinion, *New York Times Co. v. United States,* 403 U.S. 713, June 30, 1971.

[Oliver Wendell] Holmes, dissenting in a celebrated case [*Northern Securities Co. v. United States*], observed:

> Great cases like hard cases make bad law. For great cases are called great, not by reason of their real importance in shaping the law of the future, but because of some accident of immediate overwhelming interest which appeals to the feelings and distorts the judgment. These immediate interests exercise a kind of hydraulic pressure. . . .

The present cases, if not great, are at least unusual in their posture and implications, and the Holmes observation certainly has pertinent application.

A Frenetic Pace

The *New York Times* clandestinely devoted a period of three months to examining the 47 volumes that came into its unauthorized possession. Once it had begun publication of material from those volumes, the *New York* case now before us emerged. It immediately assumed, and ever since has maintained, a frenetic pace and character. Seemingly, once publication started, the material could not be made public fast enough. Seemingly, from then on, every deferral or delay, by restraint or otherwise, was abhorrent and was to be deemed violative of the First Amendment and of the public's "right immediately to know." Yet that newspaper stood before us at oral argument and professed criticism of the Government for not lodging its protest earlier than by a Monday telegram following the initial Sunday publication.

The District of Columbia case [against the *Washington Post*] is much the same.

Two federal district courts, two United States courts of appeals, and this Court—within a period of less than three weeks from inception until today—have been pressed into hurried decision of profound constitutional issues on inadequately developed and largely assumed facts without the careful deliberation that, one would hope, should characterize the American judicial process. There has been much writing about the law and little knowledge and less digestion of the facts. In the *New York* case the judges, both trial and appellate, had not yet examined the basic material when the case was brought here. In the District of Columbia case, little more was done, and what was accomplished in this respect was only on required remand, with the *Washington Post,* on the excuse that it was trying to protect its source of information, initially refusing to reveal what material it actually possessed, and with the District Court forced to make assumptions as to that possession.

With such respect as may be due to the contrary view, this, in my opinion, is not the way to try a lawsuit of this magnitude and asserted importance. It is not the way for federal courts to adjudicate, and to be required to adjudicate, issues that allegedly concern the Nation's vital welfare. The country would be none the worse off were the cases tried quickly, to be sure, but in the customary and properly deliberative manner. The most recent of the material, it is said, dates no later than 1968, already about three years ago, and the *Times* itself took three months to formulate its plan of procedure and, thus, deprived its public for that period.

A Necessary Balance

The First Amendment, after all, is only one part of an entire Constitution. Article II of the great document vests in the Executive Branch primary power over the conduct of foreign affairs and places in that branch the responsibility for the Nation's safety. Each provision of the Constitution is important, and I cannot subscribe to a doctrine of unlimited absolutism for the First Amendment at the cost of downgrading other provisions. First Amendment absolutism has never commanded a majority of this Court. See, for example, *Near v. Minnesota* (1931), and *Schenck v. United States* (1919). What is needed here is a weighing, upon properly developed standards, of the broad right of the press to print and of the very narrow right of the Government to prevent. Such standards are not yet developed. The parties here are in disagreement as to what those standards should be. But even the newspapers concede that there are situations where restraint is in order and is constitutional. Mr. Justice Holmes gave us a suggestion when he said in *Schenck,*

> It is a question of proximity and degree. When a nation is at war many things that might be said in time of peace are such a hindrance to its effort that their utterance will not be endured so long as men fight and that no Court could regard them as protected by any constitutional right.

I therefore would remand these cases to be developed expeditiously, of course, but on a schedule permitting the orderly presentation of evidence from both sides, with the use of discovery, if necessary, as authorized by the rules, and with the preparation of briefs, oral argument, and court opinions of a quality better than has been seen to this point. In making this last statement, I criticize no lawyer or judge. I know from past personal experience the agony of time pressure in the preparation of litigation. But these cases and the issues involved and the courts, including this one, deserve better than has been produced thus far.

It may well be that if these cases were allowed to develop as they should be developed, and to be tried as lawyers should try them and as courts should hear them, free of pressure and panic and sensationalism, other light would be shed on the situation and contrary considerations, for me, might prevail. But that is not the present posture of the litigation.

The Court, however, decides the cases today the other way. I therefore add one final comment.

Press Responsibilities

I strongly urge, and sincerely hope, that these two newspapers will be fully aware of their ultimate responsibilities to the United States of America. Judge Wilkey, dissenting in the *District of Columbia* case, after a review of only the affidavits before his court (the basic papers had not then been made available by either party), concluded that there were a number of examples of documents that, if in the possession of the Post, and if published, "could clearly result in great harm to the nation," and he defined "harm" to mean "the death of soldiers, the destruction of alliances, the greatly increased difficulty of negotiation with our enemies, the inability of our diplomats to negotiate. . . ." I, for one, have now been able to give at least some cursory study not only to the affidavits, but to the material itself. I regret to say that from this examination I fear that Judge Wilkey's statements have possible foundation. I therefore share his concern. I hope that damage has not already been done. If, however, damage has been done, and if, with the Court's action today, these newspapers proceed to publish the critical documents and there results therefrom "the death of soldiers, the destruction of alliances, the greatly increased difficulty of negotiation with our enemies, the inability of our diplomats to negotiate," to which list I might add the factors of prolongation of the war and of further delay in the freeing of United States prisoners, then the Nation's people will know where the responsibility for these sad consequences rests.

"There is some hope that the publication of the Pentagon Papers may make the citizenry ask questions that could prevent another Vietnam [War]."

Underscoring the Importance of a Free Press

A.M. Rosenthal

In the Pentagon Papers case, the government was found to be unable to bar the New York Times *from publishing top-secret documents pertaining to the Vietnam War. In the viewpoint that follows,* New York Times *managing editor A.M. Rosenthal contends that the case highlighted thorny First Amendment questions and allowed the public to hear the truth about its government's motives in joining the war. Writing a year after the 1971 Supreme Court decision, Rosenthal expresses hope that disclosure of the documents may prompt citizens to inquire about conflicts in the future, possibly preventing another war like Vietnam. Countering claims that the government and its military efforts would suffer as a result of the report's being published, Rosenthal maintains that the real danger lay in the government's attempt to suppress it.*

It was a year ago, on a Sunday [in 1971], that *The New York Times* began printing a series it called, with an agonizingly demure attempt to avoid sensationalism, "Vietnam Archive." Nobody paid any attention.

The journalistic world of the United States slept sweetly and soundly that June Sunday. But by Monday noon, we had all the attention we wanted and an awful lot more. Newspapermen dearly love writing about national controversy but

A.M. Rosenthal, "What a Free Press Is All About," *New York Times,* June 11, 1972, p. E6. Copyright © 1972 by The New York Times Company. Reproduced by permission.

feel a little put out when they are the controversy—something like the farmer being milked by the cow.

We knew we were devoting quite a bit of space to what everybody began calling the Pentagon Papers. (We had thought of calling it that in the beginning but somehow it sounded a little bit like what was in that pumpkin.) But those forty-eight and a half forbidding looking pages of *The Times* amounted to a news brief compared to what has been written and said about the papers since.

And it will continue. The books are beginning to come out, the trial of Daniel Ellsberg [who leaked the report] has not yet begun in Los Angeles; in Boston, Federal prosecutors are trying to find for a Grand Jury a crime to pin on prechosen culprits. . . .

Blood-and-Bone Issues

So very much has been written about the decisions involved and yet, as all newspapermen know happens often, the essence has not been written. The essence is this: Three times the reporters, editors, executives of *The Times* had placed before them, in one big bundle that simply would not go away, all those blood-and-bone issues that people spend lifetimes evading.

In the bundle were the meaning of true patriotism and national interest; the meaning and purpose of a profession, a lifetime; the meaning, duties, obligations of a free press; fear for self, for career, for the future of a newspaper; the need to see clearly what was judgment, what was ego, what was morality. As somebody said, except for sex, there it all was.

The necessity of making three decisions made the bundle appear and reappear: to publish the story; to publish the documents, which were vital to history but which would clearly heighten the attack on the paper; to refuse to accept the Attorney General's demand to cease publication.

Washington Post *employee William Frazee declares victory after hearing the Supreme Court's decision to allow newspapers to resume publication of the Pentagon Papers.* © Bettmann/CORBIS

The decisions were taken and two great issues immediately confronted the Government, the press, the courts and the public. There was, to begin with, the issue of the papers themselves and what they showed about the process of government, how decisions are made—or, sometimes more important, not made—and how the country went step by step into the most divisive foreign war in its history.

Examining Press Freedoms

And there was the great constitutional issue of freedom of the press: Does it have limits, and, if so, what are they and who determines them and can they be imposed in advance of publication? Both issues were hard and bitterly fought out in the press and in the courts.

The decisions were not taken for reasons sometimes put forward by those who agreed with *The Times* or those who thought it was dead wrong. (We learned, of course, that there were those quite as patriotic, quite as moral, quite as wise as we who felt we had made a great error; some turned against the paper forever, some are still friends and readers, a few even changed their minds.)

The decisions were not taken to change history or to try to affix blame or as an act of civil disobedience—quite the contrary, we were convinced we were acting totally within the law, and from the beginning agreed that if it did come to a court test, we would fight all the way through the judicial process but would not defy the courts.

The decisions were taken simply because we believed that this was what the national interest and the role of a free press were all about.

After a year, there still are some questions to be pondered—what happened as the result of publication of the papers, what did it all add up to?

Overblown Claims

Some interesting things the Government said would happen simply did not. It seems so long ago. Remember?

Codes would be broken. Military security endangered. Foreign governments would be afraid to deal with us. There would be nothing secret left and the Government could not move for fear of having intricate diplomatic steps made public. The people would lose confidence in government, and inside government confidentiality would be destroyed.

The electronic code machines hum away. No country seems to have pulled its embassy out of Washington. President [Richard] Nixon is at the zenith of his diplomatic endeavors and is received more happily in Peking [China] and Moscow [Russia] than any militant pacifist. No one single instance of military security damage has been surfaced. [National security adviser] Henry Kissinger manages to travel to the Soviet Union and China and Paris when reporters think he's at his desk in Washington. And as far as faith in government is concerned, if the Pentagon Papers affected Mr. Nixon's standing in the country, you certainly can't prove it by the polls on popularity or conduct of the war.

Some unpleasant things happened, not because of the publication of the papers but because the Government rushed into battle against them.

The Significance of the Pentagon Papers

By far the most important was that for the first time, a Government of the United States asked for and courts granted an injunction against newspapers—and prior restraint, death to a free press, had a precedent.

That was a loss and it could only be redressed in the future by the determination of American society—the press, the public, the courts, the politicians—to fight to the end against any future attempts at prior restraint.

No press ever remained free by bowing to censorship beforehand for fear of what might take place if it printed the truth.

But, then, what has been the result, what did it really all add up to? The answer, now, as when the decisions were made, lies not in what people said or thought about the Pentagon Papers but in the papers themselves.

For the first time in history citizens were able to read and judge and draw their conclusions from a documented case study of how one American Government after another, in concealment from its public, went to war—first into a guerrilla war, then into a great land war, then into the most massive bombardment war in history.

They could read how one Administration was locked into decisions by a previous Administration and never quite realized it; how geopolitical assumptions that could cost millions of lives were made, carried out, but never re-examined; how government officials knew that every escalating step had failed but kept this knowledge secret from the public; how secrecy had become a way of life for decision-makers and that even they never quite realized it.

It is too late to rewrite the history of the Vietnam war. But at least there is some hope that the publication of the Pentagon Papers may make the citizenry ask questions that could prevent another Vietnam. It may even make officials aware of the traps that lie waiting for men in power, including the officials of the Nixon Administration, which had quite forgotten about the Pentagon Papers until June 13, 1971.

"Fifty or sixty percent of the public 'would embrace government controls of some kind on free speech.'"

Americans Fail to Value Their Free Press

Charles Lewis

In 1971 the Supreme Court declared in New York Times Co. v. United States *that the press could not be prevented from printing a secret government report detailing U.S. involvement in the Vietnam War. Although this appeared to be a victory for the press in wartime, Charles Lewis argues in the following selection that the media have been regularly censored since then. During the War on Terror, for example, citizens have been unconcerned that the government has attempted to practice prior restraint, Lewis states. Even more concerning, he avers, are polls indicating that roughly half of Americans support press censorship in wartime, when the open flow of information is especially important. Lewis is executive director of the Center for Public Integrity, a nonpartisan organization with a focus on ethics and public policy issues.*

The tension between power and the press, between spinning and searching for truth, between disinformation and information, is of course endemic to the human condition itself. And in trying times like these, when it occasionally looks like things are going to hell, it is strangely consoling to recall that actually others before us also have traveled on what must have seemed to be the road to perdition.

For example, [in 1971,] a President [Richard Nixon] and his administration were prosecuting a difficult, unpopular war thousands of miles away on foreign soil [in Vietnam], keenly attempting without great success to control the media's access to information, particularly of the unfavorable kind. Two newspapers, the *New York Times* and the *Washington Post,* each began publishing a leaked, secret Defense Department history of the Vietnam War that dramatically revealed government deception and incompetence. The Nixon administration went into federal court against the two news organizations, separately, and, citing national security and charging treason, managed to halt publication of the "Pentagon Papers" until the U.S. Supreme Court, on June 30, 1971, sided with the First Amendment by a vote of 6-3.

While *Washington Post* executive editor Ben Bradlee was, among others, understandably exultant and relieved, he also recognized, as Bradlee later recalled in his memoir, *A Good Life,* that he had just stared into the abyss: "For the first time in the history of the American republic, newspapers had been restrained by the government from publishing a story—a black mark in the history of democracy. . . . What the hell was going on in this country that this could happen?"

Certainly a common refrain among many journalists *these* days as well, but to finish the flashback, the Pentagon Papers episode obviously was just the beginning. Bradlee at the time did not know the answer to his own question, except that "the Cold War dominated our society, and . . . the Nixon-Agnew administration was playing hardball." While Vietnam wore on for a few more years, Richard Nixon seethed and the White House siege mentality worsened.

Bleak Moments

Two days before the historic Supreme Court case, the whistle-blower who had leaked the Pentagon Papers, Daniel Ellsberg, was indicted on federal charges of conspiracy, espionage, theft of government property and the unauthorized possession of "documents and writing related to the national defense." The day after the high court decision, White House Special Counsel Charles Colson asked former CIA operative E. Howard Hunt whether "we should go down the line to nail the guy [Ellsberg] cold."

The Pentagon Papers obsession spawned the White House Special Investigations Unit, the infamous "Plumbers" unit, who, among other misadventures, weeks later broke into Ellsberg's psychiatrist's office, looking for dirt. And the poisonous paranoia didn't stop there but extended to other burglaries, including the Democratic Party national headquarters at the Watergate complex, electronic surveillance, misuse of confidential tax return information against perceived political enemies, mail fraud, obstruction of justice and an astonishing array of other illegal government abuses of power, ultimately exposed, prosecuted and culminating in the *only* resignation of a sitting U.S. president.

The Pentagon Papers case and the Watergate scandal still represent U.S. history's high-water mark in the long-standing struggle between raw political power and democratic values, poignantly affirming the public's right to know about its government. They still represent the bleakest moments and the loftiest triumphs of journalism in contemporary America, an invaluable perspective today as we ponder the future and assess the tectonic damage to our long-cherished freedoms of speech and information in the past [four], disquieting years in the wake of the devastating, unimaginable carnage of September 11, 2001.

Suddenly, despite living in the most powerful nation on earth, we all faced a shattering if all-too-familiar realization of our own human vulnerabilities, including the quite palpable fear for our own personal safety, indelibly seared into our collective consciousness. While the Vietnam and Watergate era was quite extraordinary, most Americans, including journalists, *never* had the sense that their physical well-being was potentially at risk. Juxtapose our pervasive sense of insecurity and the patriotic and visceral, survival-related instinct to do anything to thwart "terrorism," with a President and administration which assumed power with a well-documented predisposition to tightly manage and control information, and it is not difficult to understand the current, wholesale assault on openness and government accountability today. . . .

Press Censorship Today

A month *before* September 11, the Justice Department secretly subpoenaed Associated Press reporter John Solomon's home telephone records. As Solomon, the AP deputy Washington bureau chief, told me, "The Justice Department has indicated to us that they were actually trying to stop the publication of a story that I was working on and tried to find out who I was talking to and cut off the flow of information. So it does get into the issue of prior restraint, along with First and Fourth Amendment issues."

As we all know too well, in the weeks immediately following September 11th, the Bush administration obtained passage of the USA Patriot Act, with no public debate or amendments, among other things, giving federal authorities more power to access email and telephone communications. The federal government detained hundreds of people indefinitely without releasing the most basic information about them. Attorney General John Ashcroft described the news blackout in Orwellian fashion: "It would be a violation of the privacy rights of individuals for me to create some kind of list." Usually open U.S. immigration proceedings were closed to the public, and separately, the Attorney General sent a chilling, unprecedented directive throughout the government, "When you carefully consider FOIA [Freedom of Information Act] requests and decide to withhold records, in whole or in part, you can be assured that the Department of Justice will defend your decisions. . . ." And President Bush quietly signed Executive Order 13233, overriding the post-Watergate 1978 Presidential Records Act and sharply reducing public access to the papers of former presidents, including his father's.

In the war in Afghanistan, journalists were severely limited in their access to field of action. As the Reporters Committee on Freedom of the Press noted in its excellent report, *Homeland Confidential,* "In effect, most American broadcasters and newspaper reporters scratched out coverage from Pentagon briefings, a rare interview on a U.S. aircraft carrier or a humanitarian aid airlift, or from carefully selected military videos or from leaks. . . . The truth is, the American media's vantage point for the war has never been at the frontlines with American troops."

Indeed, who can forget December 6, 2001, when Marines locked reporters and photographers in a warehouse to prevent them from covering American troops killed or injured north of Kandahar, Afghanistan? And while embedded reporters enjoyed far greater access—and danger—in Iraq, many news organizations, including the *New York Times* and the *Washington Post,* have recently been introspective or even mildly apologetic for their over-reliance on official statements in the lead-up to the war.

Most Americans No Longer Value a Free Press

But, meanwhile, it is hard to overstate the fear and paranoia of an entire, terrorized nation. Within six months of September 11th, in 300 separate instances, federal, state and local officials restricted access to government records by executive order, or proposed new laws to sharply curtail their availability, according to the National Conference of State Legislatures. More recently, sunshine activists are most alarmed about the Homeland Security Act, especially its Protected Critical Infrastructure Information (PCII) section. Former *Miami Herald* managing editor Pete Weitzel recently described it in the *American Editor* as a "black hole" for almost boundless censorship. The ranking Democrat on the Senate Judiciary Committee, Patrick Leahy, called the move—which would create an entirely new level of secrecy and a system of binding nondisclosure agreements effectively muzzling millions of state and local officials and private contractors—"the single greatest rollback of FOIA in history."

The American people unfortunately are not as informed, concerned, or supportive about this deepening crisis as they ought to be. A national poll sponsored by the *Chicago Tribune* on First Amendment issues in late June [2004] found that roughly half of the public believe there should have been some kind of "press restraint" on coverage of the Abu Ghraib prison abuse scandal in Iraq—somewhat ironic considering that the chairman of the Joint Chiefs of Staff, General Richard Myers, personally had implored CBS's *60 Minutes II* to keep its exposé off the air in the name of national security, which the network actually did voluntarily until learning that investigative reporter Seymour Hersh would be publishing the story in the *New Yorker*. In general, according to Charles Madigan, editor of the *Tribune*'s Perspective section, fifty or sixty percent of the public "would embrace government controls of some kind on free speech, particularly when it has sexual content or is heard as unpatriotic."

This ambivalence in which at least *half* of the country equates draconian security and secrecy measures with their own safety is quite serious and very possibly insurmountable. Tom Blanton, executive director of the National Security Archive in Washington wrote in *National Security and Open Government*, "The government has successfully framed the debate after 9/11 as terrorism fighters versus civil libertarians, as soldiers versus reporters, as hawks versus doves. In wartime, the poundage of the former will always outweigh the latter. . . . We need to place openness where it belongs, not only at the center of our values, but also at the center of our strategy for security."

Both the Congressional September 11th investigation and the 9/11 Commission appointed by President Bush separately documented extensive "intelligence hoarding" and petty bureaucratic turf wars inside the government, excessive secrecy for all the wrong reasons and the dire consequences of not sharing information. But beyond that, the ignorance of the body politic was anything but blissful. The 9/11 Commission concluded, "We believe American and international public opinion might have been different—and so might the range of options for a president—had they [the American people] been informed of [the growing al Qaeda danger]."

Preserving Democracy

It is a powerful message still substantially untold but essential to understanding and preserving freedom of the press as we know it. Indeed, the situation is so foreboding that the Associated Press has taken the unusual step of proposing an industry-wide lobby to "identify and oppose legislation that puts unreasonable restrictions on public information." . . .

As Supreme Court Justice Potter Stewart wrote in the Pentagon Papers case, words we should all remember, "In the absence of governmental checks and balances present in other areas of our national life, the only effective restraint upon executive policy and power in the areas of national defense and international affairs may lie in an enlightened citizenry—in an informed and critical public opinion which alone can here protect the values of democratic government."

"The press ... has retreated from the boldness it showed in 1971."

Today's Press Is Reluctant to Exercise Its Rights

Anthony Lewis

In New York Times v. United States, also called the Pentagon Papers case, the Court affirmed the press's right to challenge officials by printing classified documents regarding the Vietnam War. Yet in today's War on Terror, charges Anthony Lewis in the following excerpt, the press is no longer willing to boldly question presidential powers. Lewis offers examples of the press's reluctance to report on civil liberties violations and its failure to fully examine the government's assertions leading up to the second war with Iraq. According to Lewis, society seems to have forgotten the lesson of the Pentagon Papers case: The president is not above the law and must not be permitted to operate without checks on his power. Lewis is a former columnist for the New York Times.

Public disclosure of the Pentagon Papers challenged the core of a president's power: his role in foreign and national security affairs. Throughout the cold war, until well into the Vietnam era, virtually all of the public had been content to let presidents—of both parties—make that policy. As the Vietnam War ground on, cruelly and fruitlessly, dissent became significant. The Pentagon Papers showed us that there had all along been dissent inside the government. Thomas Powers, in an essay in *Inside the Pentagon Papers*, says that

Anthony Lewis, "More than Fit to Print," *New York Review of Books,* April 17, 2005. Copyright © 2005 by NYREV, Inc. Reproduced with permission from *The New York Review of Books.*

their disclosure "broke a kind of spell in this country, a notion that the people and the government had to always be in consensus on all the major [foreign policy] issues."

Initial Effects of the Pentagon Papers

The courts were another institution changed by the Pentagon Papers. Judges tend to defer to executive officials on issues of national security, explaining that they themselves lack necessary expertise. But here, in a case involving thousands of pages of top secret documents, they said no to hyperbolic government claims of damage that would be done if the newspapers were allowed to go on publishing—soldiers' lives lost, alliances damaged. The government's request for an injunction against publication was turned down by a federal trial judge in New York, by a trial judge and the Court of Appeals in Washington in the *Washington Post* case, and finally by the Supreme Court. Floyd Abrams, one of the assisting lawyers who went on from the *Times* case to become a leading First Amendment lawyer, has said that "the enduring lesson of the Pentagon Papers case ... is the need for the greatest caution and dubiety by the judiciary in accepting representations by the government as to the likelihood of harm."

The press was also profoundly affected by the Pentagon Papers. In the Washington of the 1950s and 1960s, correspondents and columnists shared the government's premises on the great issues of foreign policy, notably the cold war. The press believed in the good faith of officials and their superior knowledge. The Vietnam War undermined both those beliefs. The young correspondents in the field, David Halberstam and the rest, knew more about what was happening and reported it more honestly than generals and presidents. But would an establishment newspaper like the *Times* go so far as to publish thousands of pages from top secret documents about the war?

Professors Harold Edgar and Benno Schmidt Jr. of the Columbia Law School wrote that publication of the papers symbolized the passing of an era in which newsmen could be counted upon to work within reasonably well understood boundaries in disclosing information that politicians deemed sensitive.

There had been, they said, a "symbiotic relationship between politicians and the press." But

> *The New York Times,* by publishing the papers . . . demonstrated that much of the press was no longer willing to be merely an occasionally critical associate devoted to common aims, but intended to become an adversary threatening to discredit not only political dogma but also the motives of the nation's leaders. . . .

Today's Reluctant Press

Inside the Pentagon Papers tells a wonderful story, and it is a significant book today. For the effects that the Pentagon Papers controversy had on some institutions in our society seem to have worn off.

The press, for one, has retreated from the boldness it showed in 1971. *The New York Times* and *The Washington Post* have apologized for having failed adequately to examine the government's claims in the run-up to the Iraq war. The press was slow to give serious coverage to the Bush administration's assaults on civil liberty, such as the claim that the President can imprison American citizens indefinitely as alleged "enemy combatants" without trial or access to counsel. (Newspapers have more recently emerged from their torpor, for example in vigorously reporting the widespread torture of prisoners held by the US in Iraq, Guantánamo [Cuba], and Afghanistan, and the Bush administration's legal memoranda that opened the way to torture. Even there, though, some of the breakthrough reporting came from Seymour Hersh and Jane Mayer in *The New Yorker.*)

The crucial lesson of the Pentagon Papers and then Watergate was that presidents are not above the law. So we thought. But today government lawyers argue that the president *is* above the law—that he can order the torture of prisoners even though treaties and a federal law forbid it. John Yoo, a former Justice Department official who wrote some of the broad claims of presidential power in memoranda, told Jane Mayer recently that Congress does not have power to "tie the president's hands in regard to torture as an interrogation technique." The constitutional remedy for presidential abuse of his authority, he said, is impeachment. Yoo also told Ms. Mayer that the 2004 election was a "referendum" on the torture issue: the people had spoken, and the debate was over. And so, in the view of this prominent conservative legal thinker, a professor at the University of California law school in Berkeley, an election in which the torture issue was not discussed has legitimized President Bush's right to order its use.

Checks and Balances

The notion that we have a plebiscitary democracy in this country would have astonished James Madison and the other Framers of the Constitution, who thought they were establishing a federal republic of limited powers. So would the idea that the president can ignore laws passed by Congress. One of the fundamental constitutional checks against abuse of power, as the Framers saw it, was the separation of powers in three branches of the federal government: executive, legislative, judicial. If one overreached, they thought, another would curb its abuse.

Congress as an institution has hardly exercised its checking power since the terrorist attacks of September 11, 2001. It gave President Bush greatly expanded investigative and prosecutorial authority in the Patriot Act. It has only intermittently challenged the unprecedented secrecy he has imposed on government activity.

That leaves the third branch, the courts. In the context of the "war on terrorism," would they decide a case like the Pentagon Papers the same way today? No one can be sure. But lately there have been signs that judges are unwilling to be cowed by the claims, made since September 11, of unreviewable presidential power. The Supreme Court ruled [in 2004] that citizens held without trial as "enemy combatants" must have an opportunity to answer official suspicions, and held that prisoners at Guantánamo Bay may file petitions in federal courts for release on habeas corpus.

The Supreme Court made its decision on citizens held without trial in the case of Yaser Esam Hamdi. Rather than tell him its reasons for holding him and letting him answer, the government sent Hamdi back to his home in Saudi Arabia. Then, [in early 2005], a federal district judge in South Carolina ordered the release of the other American held as an "enemy combatant," Jose Padilla. The judge—Henry F. Floyd, nominated by President Bush in 2003—said: "The court finds that the president has no power, neither express nor implied, neither constitutional nor statutory, to hold petitioner as an enemy combatant." To allow that, Judge Floyd said,

> would not only offend the rule of law and violate this country's tradition, but it would also be a betrayal of this nation's commitment to the separation of powers that safeguards our democratic values and individual liberties.

It was only a trial judge speaking, and officials immediately said they would appeal. His decision affected one American citizen while mistreatment of prisoners overseas during interrogation, as FBI reports among other things have shown, remains inadequately investigated, much less forbidden. But that a trial judge reached those conclusions, and had the courage to express them, meant something. Perhaps, in the courts, the spirit of the Pentagon Papers lives.

Chapter 4

According Due
Process Rights to
Enemy Combatants

Case Overview

Yaser Esam Hamdi et al. v. Donald H. Rumsfeld et al. (2004)

In a system of coordinated attacks on U.S. landmarks, terrorists killed nearly three thousand people on September 11,
2001. Responding to the nation's fear of further violence,
Congress authorized the president to "use all necessary and
appropriate force" against anyone who aided the terrorist attacks. With the War on Terror in full force, American citizen
Yaser Hamdi was arrested in a zone of active combat in Afghanistan and transferred to a U.S. military prison. He was
designated as an enemy combatant, which, according to the
government, meant that he could be detained until the end of
hostilities without consulting a lawyer and without being
charged with a crime. When Hamdi claimed this treatment
was in violation of his constitutional right to due process, the
government countered that his detention was not intended as
a punishment but as a protection against his aiding in acts of
terrorism against the United States or rejoining the enemy on
the battlefield. Moreover, officials stated that they did not wish
to burden the military with hearings during a time of war.

A year after Hamdi was arrested, a district court reviewed
the only evidence the government had produced against
Hamdi: a declaration by a government official explaining how
Hamdi came to be labeled as an enemy combatant. In the district court's contention, the declaration fell "far short" of supporting the detention. The court ordered the government to
turn over further evidence, for only then, the court said, could
it conduct "meaningful judicial review" of whether Hamdi's
detention was legal.

The U.S. Court of Appeals for the Fourth Circuit disagreed with the district court. It maintained that the lower
court had failed to appropriately consider the government's
security and intelligence interests. In particular, it believed

that judicial review in enemy combatant cases jeopardized national security by exposing classified information in court. The Fourth Circuit also declared that the detaining of uncharged suspects fell within the war powers given the executive branch in the Constitution.

When the case reached the Supreme Court, it produced several opinions, none of which captured the majority. The plurality opinion stated that there is no law against the government holding a U.S. citizen as an enemy combatant (defined in this case as a person who is "part of or supporting forces hostile to," and "engaged in an armed conflict against," the United States). However, the Court asserted that the government should have notified Hamdi of the factual basis for his classification as an enemy combatant, given him an opportunity to refute the assertions before a neutral decision maker, and allowed him to be represented by an attorney. Granting these rights to citizens, reasoned the Supreme Court, would not harm the government's war efforts.

The Court added, however, that in the interest of national defense it may be necessary in the hearings to allow evidence that would not be considered reliable in regular court, such as hearsay. Moreover, it noted, the burden of proof that normally lies with the prosecution may need to be shifted to the enemy combatant. In this way the defendant would not necessarily be considered innocent until proven guilty. Shortly following the decision, the Department of Defense developed a military tribunal to serve as the neutral decision maker in future cases although some critics felt that the military tribunal would not be neutral.

After nearly three years Hamdi was released and deported in exchange for renouncing his U.S. citizenship and agreeing not to return to the United States or to travel to an extensive list of countries known for terrorist activity. Commentators continue to debate whether his case was an important victory for, or was a grave blow to, civil liberties in wartime.

> "The risk of erroneous deprivation of a citizen's liberty in the absence of sufficient [due] process here is very real."

The Court's Decision: Detained U.S. Citizens Must Be Granted Due Process

Sandra Day O'Connor

In 2001 Yaser Hamdi, an American citizen, was captured during hostilities in Afghanistan, presumably fighting against the United States. Designating him as an enemy combatant in the War on Terror, the military held him for almost three years without charging him with a crime or allowing him access to legal counsel. In the following excerpt from Hamdi v. Rumsfeld, *justice Sandra Day O'Connor expresses the Court's opinion that American citizens may be detained as enemy combatants until the end of the war but must be given a meaningful factual hearing before a neutral decision maker. This requirement strikes a proper balance between the constitutional rights of the accused, the Court contends, and the needs of the wartime government to maintain national defense secrecy and keep enemies off the battlefield. O'Connor, the first female Supreme Court justice, served from 1981 to 2005.*

On September 11, 2001, the al Qaeda terrorist network used hijacked commercial airliners to attack prominent targets in the United States. Approximately 3,000 people were killed in those attacks. One week later, in response to these "acts of treacherous violence," Congress passed a resolution [Authorization for Use of Military Force (AUMF)] authorizing the President to "use all necessary and appropriate force

Sandra Day O'Connor, plurality opinion, *Hamdi v. Rumsfeld*, 03-6696, June 28, 2004.

against those nations, organizations, or persons he determines planned, authorized, committed, or aided the terrorist attacks" or "harbored such organizations or persons, in order to prevent any future acts of international terrorism against the United States by such nations, organizations or persons." Soon thereafter, the President ordered United States Armed Forces to Afghanistan, with a mission to subdue al Qaeda and quell the Taliban regime that was known to support it.

Charges of Rights Violations

This case arises out of the detention of a man whom the Government alleges took up arms with the Taliban during this conflict. His name is Yaser Esam Hamdi. Born an American citizen in Louisiana in 1980, Hamdi moved with his family to Saudi Arabia as a child. By 2001, the parties agree, he resided in Afghanistan. At some point that year, he was seized by members of the Northern Alliance, a coalition of military groups opposed to the Taliban government, and eventually was turned over to the United States military. The Government asserts that it initially detained and interrogated Hamdi in Afghanistan before transferring him to the United States Naval Base in Guantanamo Bay in January 2002. In April 2002, upon learning that Hamdi is an American citizen, authorities transferred him to a naval brig in Norfolk, Virginia, where he remained until a recent transfer to a brig in Charleston, South Carolina. The Government contends that Hamdi is an "enemy combatant," and that this status justifies holding him in the United States indefinitely—without formal charges or proceedings—unless and until it makes the determination that access to counsel or further process is warranted.

In June 2002, Hamdi's father, Esam Fouad Hamdi, filed the present petition for a writ of habeas corpus in the Eastern District of Virginia, naming as petitioners his son and himself as next friend. The elder Hamdi alleges in the petition that he has had no contact with his son since the Government took custody of him in 2001, and that the Government has held his son "without access to legal counsel or notice of any charges pending against him." The petition contends that Hamdi's detention was not legally authorized. It argues that, "as an American citizen, . . . Hamdi enjoys the full protections of the Constitution," and that Hamdi's detention in the United States without charges, access to an impartial tribunal, or assistance of counsel "violated and continue[s] to violate the Fifth and Fourteenth Amendments to the United States Constitution." The habeas petition asks that the court, among other things, (1) appoint counsel for Hamdi; (2) order respondents to cease interrogating him; (3) declare that he is being held in violation of the Fifth and Fourteenth Amendments; (4) "to the extent Respondents contest any material factual allegations in this Petition, schedule an evidentiary hearing, at which Petitioners may adduce proof in support of their allegations"; and (5) order that Hamdi be released from his "unlawful custody." . . .

The Detention of Enemy Combatants Has Been Authorized

The threshold question before us is whether the Executive has the authority to detain citizens who qualify as "enemy combatants." There is some debate as to the proper scope of this term, and the Government has never provided any court with the full criteria that it uses in classifying individuals as such. It has made clear, however, that, for purposes of this case, the "enemy combatant" that it is seeking to detain is an individual who, it alleges, was "'part of or supporting forces hostile to the United States or coalition partners'" in Afghanistan and who "'engaged in an armed conflict against the United States'" there. We therefore answer only the narrow question before us: whether the detention of citizens falling within that definition is authorized.

U.S.-born Yaser Hamdi, seen here after being captured in Afghanistan during hostilities with the Taliban, was detained for years by the U.S. military without charging him with a crime or allowing him access to legal counsel. © Reuters/CORBIS

The Government maintains that no explicit congressional authorization is required, because the Executive possesses plenary authority to detain pursuant to Article II of the Constitution. We do not reach the question whether Article II provides such authority, however, because we agree with the Government's alternative position, that Congress has in fact authorized Hamdi's detention, through the AUMF. . . .

Hamdi and Due Process Rights

It is beyond question that substantial interests lie on both sides of the scale in this case. Hamdi's . . . is the most elemental of liberty interests—the interest in being free from physical detention by one's own government. [According to the Court in] *Foucha v. Louisiana* (1992), "Freedom from bodily restraint has always been at the core of the liberty protected by the Due Process Clause from arbitrary governmental action." [In *United States v. Salerno* (1987) it said,] "In our society liberty is the norm," and detention without trial "is the carefully limited exception." [In *Foucha* the Court asserted,] "We have always been careful not to 'minimize the importance and fundamental nature' of the individual's right to liberty," and we will not do so today.

Nor is the weight on this side of the scale offset by the circumstances of war or the accusation of treasonous behavior, for [according to *Jones v. United States* (1983),] "it is clear that commitment for *any* purpose constitutes a significant deprivation of liberty that requires due process protection," and at this stage . . . we consider the interest of the *erroneously* detained individual. [See] *Carey v. Piphus* (1978): "Procedural due process rules are meant to protect persons not from the deprivation, but from the mistaken or unjustified deprivation of life, liberty, or property." [The case also notes,] "the importance to organized society that procedural due process be observed," and [emphasizes] that "the right to procedural due process is 'absolute' in the sense that it does not depend upon the merits of a claimant's substantive assertions." Indeed, as *amicus* briefs from media and relief organizations emphasize, the risk of erroneous deprivation of a citizen's liberty in the absence of sufficient process here is very real. . . . We reaffirm today the fundamental nature of a citizen's right to be free from involuntary confinement by his own government without due process of law, and we weigh the opposing governmental interests against the curtailment of liberty that such confinement entails.

The Government and National Security Concerns

On the other side of the scale are the weighty and sensitive governmental interests in ensuring that those who have in fact fought with the enemy during a war do not return to battle against the United States. The law of war and the realities of combat may render such detentions both necessary and appropriate, and our due process analysis need not blink at those realities. Without doubt, our Constitution recognizes that core strategic matters of warmaking belong in the hands of those who are best positioned and most politically accountable for making them. *Department of Navy v. Egan* (1988) [notes] the reluctance of the courts "to intrude upon the authority of the Executive in military and national security affairs"; *Youngstown Sheet & Tube Co. v. Sawyer* (1952) [acknowledges] "broad powers in military commanders engaged in day-to-day fighting in a theater of war."

The Government also argues at some length that its interests in reducing the process available to alleged enemy combatants are heightened by the practical difficulties that would accompany a system of trial-like process. In its view, military officers who are engaged in the serious work of waging battle would be unnecessarily and dangerously distracted by litigation half a world away, and discovery into military operations would both intrude on the sensitive secrets of national defense and result in a futile search for evidence buried under the rubble of war. . . .

Balancing Dual Interests

We believe that neither the process proposed by the Government nor the process apparently envisioned by the District Court strikes the proper constitutional balance when a United States citizen is detained in the United States as an enemy combatant. That is, "the risk of erroneous deprivation" of a detainee's liberty interest is unacceptably high. . . .

We therefore hold that a citizen-detainee seeking to challenge his classification as an enemy combatant must receive notice of the factual basis for his classification, and a fair opportunity to rebut the Government's factual assertions before a neutral decisionmaker. See *Cleveland Bd. of Ed. v. Loudermill* (1985): "An essential principle of due process is that a deprivation of life, liberty, or property 'be preceded by notice and opportunity for hearing appropriate to the nature of the case.'" "For more than a century the central meaning of procedural due process has been clear: 'Parties whose rights are to be affected are entitled to be heard; and in order that they may enjoy that right they must first be notified.' It is equally fundamental that the right to notice and an opportunity to be heard 'must be granted at a meaningful time and in a meaningful manner,'" [according to] *Fuentes v. Shevin* (1972). These essential constitutional promises may not be eroded.

At the same time, the exigencies of the circumstances may demand that, aside from these core elements, enemy combatant proceedings may be tailored to alleviate their uncommon potential to burden the Executive at a time of ongoing military conflict. Hearsay, for example, may need to be accepted as the most reliable available evidence from the Government in such a proceeding. Likewise, the Constitution would not be offended by a presumption in favor of the Government's evidence, so long as that presumption remained a rebuttable one and fair opportunity for rebuttal were provided. Thus, once the Government puts forth credible evidence that the habeas petitioner meets the enemy-combatant criteria, the onus could shift to the petitioner to rebut that evidence with more persuasive evidence that he falls outside the criteria. A burden-shifting scheme of this sort would meet the goal of ensuring that the errant tourist, embedded journalist, or local aid worker has a chance to prove military error while giving due regard to the Executive once it has put forth meaningful support for its conclusion that the detainee is in fact an enemy combatant. In the words of *Mathews [v. Eldridge]* (1976), process of this sort would sufficiently address the "risk of erroneous deprivation" of a detainee's liberty interest while eliminating certain procedures that have questionable additional value in light of the burden on the Government.

We think it unlikely that this basic process will have the dire impact on the central functions of warmaking that the Government forecasts. The parties agree that initial captures on the battlefield need not receive the process we have discussed here; that process is due only when the determination is made to *continue* to hold those who have been seized. . . .

In sum, while the full protections that accompany challenges to detentions in other settings may prove unworkable and inappropriate in the enemy-combatant setting, the threats to military operations posed by a basic system of independent review are not so weighty as to trump a citizen's core rights to challenge meaningfully the Government's case and to be heard by an impartial adjudicator.

> "Consistent with the Due Process Clause,
> [an executive may] unilaterally decide to
> detain an individual . . . for the public
> safety even if he is mistaken."

Dissenting Opinion: Due Process Rights May Be Restricted in Wartime

Clarence Thomas

During the War on Terror, the United States arrested American citizen Yaser Hamdi and held him at length without charging him with a crime, holding a hearing, or allowing him to speak with a lawyer. Although this detention appears to be unconstitutional, it does comport with the due process clause of the Constitution, argues Justice Clarence Thomas in his following dissent in Hamdi v. Rumsfeld *(2004). In the interest of national security, the Court should not expect full disclosure from the executive branch regarding enemy combatants, Thomas insists. Nor should it grant all suspects access to counsel, he maintains, because that would hinder the government's ability to gather intelligence from enemy suspects. In fact, Thomas claims, the Court lacks the authority to question the federal government's wartime decisions. Thomas has served on the Court since 1991.*

The Executive Branch, acting pursuant to the powers vested in the President by the Constitution and with explicit congressional approval, has determined that Yaser Hamdi is an enemy combatant and should be detained. This detention falls squarely within the Federal Government's war powers, and we lack the expertise and capacity to second-guess that decision. As such, petitioners' habeas challenge should fail, and there is

Clarence Thomas, dissenting opinion, *Hamdi v. Rumsfeld*, 03-6696, June 28, 2004.

no reason to remand the case. The plurality reaches a contrary conclusion by failing adequately to consider basic principles of the constitutional structure as it relates to national security and foreign affairs. . . .

"It is 'obvious and unarguable' that no governmental interest is more compelling than the security of the Nation," [said the Court in] *Haig v. Agee* (1981). The national security, after all, is the primary responsibility and purpose of the Federal Government. See The Federalist No. 23: "The principle purposes to be answered by Union are these—The common defence of the members—the preservation of the public peace as well against internal convulsions as external attacks." But because the Founders understood that they could not foresee the myriad potential threats to national security that might later arise, they chose to create a Federal Government that necessarily possesses sufficient power to handle any threat to the security of the Nation. [The Federalist No. 23 maintains that] the power to protect the Nation

> ought to exist without limitation . . . *because it is impossible to foresee or define the extent and variety of national exigencies, or the correspondent extent & variety of the means which may be necessary to satisfy them.* The circumstances that endanger the safety of nations are infinite; and for this reason no constitutional shackles can wisely be imposed on the power to which the care of it is committed.

The Founders intended that the President have primary responsibility—along with the necessary power—to protect the national security and to conduct the Nation's foreign relations. . . .

Presidential Authority

This Court has long . . . held that the President has *constitutional* authority to protect the national security and that this authority carries with it broad discretion. [According to *Prize Cases,*]

> If a war be made by invasion of a foreign nation, the President is not only authorized but bound to resist force by force. He does not initiate the war, but is bound to accept the challenge without waiting for any special legislative authority. . . . Whether the President in fulfilling his duties, as Commander in-chief, in suppressing an insurrection, has met with such armed hostile resistance . . . is a question to be decided *by him*.

The Court has acknowledged [in *Fleming v. Page* (1850)] that the President has the authority to "employ [the Nation's Armed Forces] in the manner he may deem most effectual to harass and conquer and subdue the enemy." With respect to foreign affairs as well, the Court has recognized the President's independent authority and need to be free from interference. . . .

Congress, to be sure, has a substantial and essential role in both foreign affairs and national security. But it is crucial to recognize that *judicial* interference in these domains destroys the purpose of vesting primary responsibility in a unitary Executive. I cannot improve on Justice [Robert] Jackson's words, speaking for the Court:

> The President, both as Commander-in-Chief and as the Nation's organ for foreign affairs, has available intelligence services whose reports are not and ought not to be published to the world. It would be intolerable that courts, without the relevant information, should review and perhaps nullify actions of the Executive taken on information properly held secret. Nor can courts sit *in camera* in order to be taken into executive confidences. But even if courts could require full disclosure, the very nature of executive decisions as to foreign policy is political, not judicial. Such decisions are wholly confided by our Constitution to the political departments of the government, Executive and Legislative. They are delicate, complex, and involve large elements of prophecy. They are and should be undertaken only by those directly responsible to the people whose welfare

they advance or imperil. They are decisions of a kind for which the Judiciary has neither aptitude, facilities nor responsibility and which has long been held to belong in the domain of political power not subject to judicial intrusion or inquiry. . . .

No Second-Guessing

I agree with the plurality that the Federal Government has power to detain those that the Executive Branch determines to be enemy combatants. But I do not think that the plurality has adequately explained the breadth of the President's authority to detain enemy combatants, an authority that includes making virtually conclusive factual findings. In my view, . . . we lack the capacity and responsibility to second-guess this determination.

This makes complete sense once the process that is due Hamdi is made clear. As an initial matter, it is possible that the Due Process Clause requires only "that our Government must proceed according to the 'law of the land'—that is, according to written constitutional and statutory provisions," [as suggested by Justice Hugo Black] *In re Winship* (1970). I need not go this far today because the Court has already explained the nature of due process in this context.

In a case strikingly similar to this one [*Moyer v. Peabody* (1909)], the Court addressed a Governor's authority to detain for an extended period a person the executive believed to be responsible, in part, for a local insurrection. Justice [Oliver Wendell] Holmes wrote for a unanimous Court:

> When it comes to a decision by the head of the State upon a matter involving its life, the ordinary rights of individuals must yield to what *he deems* the necessities of the moment. Public danger warrants the substitution of executive process for judicial process. This was admitted with regard to killing men in the actual clash of arms, and we think it obvious, although it was disputed, that the same is true of temporary detention to prevent apprehended harm.

The Court answered Moyer's claim that he had been denied due process by emphasizing that

> it is familiar that what is due process of law depends on circumstances. It varies with the subject-matter and the necessities of the situation. Thus summary proceedings suffice for taxes, and executive decisions for exclusion from the country.... Such arrests are not necessarily for punishment, but are by way of precaution to prevent the exercise of hostile power.

In this context, due process requires nothing more than a good-faith executive determination. To be clear: The Court has held that an executive, acting pursuant to statutory and constitutional authority may, consistent with the Due Process Clause, unilaterally decide to detain an individual if the executive deems this necessary for the public safety *even if he is mistaken.* . . .

Accordingly, I conclude that the Government's detention of Hamdi as an enemy combatant does not violate the Constitution. By detaining Hamdi, the President, in the prosecution of a war and authorized by Congress, has acted well within his authority. Hamdi thereby received all the process to which he was due under the circumstances. I therefore believe that this is no occasion to balance the competing interests, as the plurality unconvincingly attempts to do. . . .

National Security Is Most Important

At issue here is the far more significant interest of the security of the Nation. The Government seeks to further that interest by detaining an enemy soldier not only to prevent him from rejoining the ongoing fight. Rather, as the Government explains, detention can serve to gather critical intelligence regarding the intentions and capabilities of our adversaries, a function that the Government avers has become all the more important in the war on terrorism.

Additional process, the Government explains, will destroy the intelligence gathering function. It also does seem quite likely that, under the process envisioned by the plurality, various military officials will have to take time to litigate this matter. And though the plurality does not say so, a meaningful ability to challenge the Government's factual allegations will probably require the Government to divulge highly classified information to the purported enemy combatant, who might then upon release return to the fight armed with our most closely held secrets. . . .

Undeniably, Hamdi has been deprived of a serious interest, one actually protected by the Due Process Clause. Against this, however, is the Government's overriding interest in protecting the Nation. If a deprivation of liberty can be justified by the need to protect a town, the protection of the Nation, *a fortiori*, justifies it.

I acknowledge that under the plurality's approach, it might, at times, be appropriate to give detainees access to counsel and notice of the factual basis for the Government's determination. But properly accounting for the Government's interests also requires concluding that access to counsel and to the factual basis would not always be warranted. Though common sense suffices, the Government thoroughly explains that counsel would often destroy the intelligence gathering function. Equally obvious is the Government's interest in not fighting the war in its own courts . . . and protecting classified information. . . .

For these reasons, I would affirm the judgment of the Court of Appeals.

"The case is a significant victory for civil liberties because ... even a citizen arrested on a foreign battlefield must be given a meaningful factual hearing."

The *Hamdi* Decision Defends Civil Liberties

Erwin Chemerinsky

Yaser Hamdi was arrested in Afghanistan in 2001 and held as an enemy combatant for allegedly fighting against the United States in the War on Terror. In June 2004 the Supreme Court ruled that as an American citizen, Hamdi had a constitutional right to a hearing, which he had been denied. In the viewpoint that follows, Erwin Chemerinsky, a Duke law professor, extols the decision, which he says preserves the civil liberties of not only Hamdi but of all Americans. Had the Court accepted the argument that the government had unreviewable authority to detain enemy combatants without charging them, he cautions, the government would be free to arrest and hold anyone without according them due process.

In three recent cases [decided in June 2004], the Supreme Court emphatically upheld the rule of law and the rights of people detained as part of the war on terrorism:

- In *Rasul v. Bush,* the Court affirmed the rights of detainees at [U.S. Naval base] Guantanamo Bay, Cuba, to have their habeas corpus petitions heard in federal court.

- In *Hamdi v. Rumsfeld,* the Court concluded that a U.S. citizen apprehended in a foreign country and held as an

Erwin Chemerinsky, "Three Decisions, One Big Victory for Civil Rights," *Trial,* vol. 74, September 2004, pp. 74–77. Copyright © 2004 by The Association of Trial Lawyers of America. Reproduced by permission.

enemy combatant was entitled to due process and a meaningful factual hearing.

- In *Rumsfeld v. Padilla,* the Court dismissed on jurisdictional grounds a challenge by an American citizen apprehended in the United States and held as an enemy combatant, ruling that Jose Padilla must sue in federal court in South Carolina, where he is being held, rather than in New York, where his case was litigated. But at least five justices clearly signaled that had they reached the merits of the case, they would have ruled in Padilla's favor and held that the government has no authority to detain an American citizen arrested in the United States as an enemy combatant.

The significance of these cases can be appreciated only by understanding the Bush administration's position. In both the Supreme Court and the lower federal courts, the government claimed it had unreviewable authority to hold enemy combatants as part of the war on terrorism. In its briefs and oral arguments to the Supreme Court, the solicitor general's office said the president had inherent authority to detain individuals as enemy combatants and that the courts had no power to review such detentions. In *Padilla,* for example, Deputy Solicitor General Paul Clement said in oral argument before the Court that the only hearing an alleged enemy combatant is entitled to is answering questions in an interrogation.

If the Supreme Court had accepted these arguments, nothing could keep the government from arresting literally anyone and holding the person without due process. Under the government's position, even if the Guantanamo detainees were horribly tortured, no court could hear their claims. But the Supreme Court forcefully rejected this argument, ruling that courts can review detentions—even of detainees in the war on terrorism. . . .

A Fractured Court in *Hamdi v. Rumsfeld*

Yaser Hamdi was arrested in Afghanistan and brought to Guantanamo Bay. There authorities discovered that he was a U.S. citizen and sent him to a military prison in South Carolina. He has been held ever since as an enemy combatant, without having been charged with any crime. His situation is identical to that of John Walker Lindh, the "American Taliban," except that Walker Lindh was indicted and pleaded guilty to crimes.

The Fourth Circuit agreed with the government that Hamdi was not entitled to any form of due process or judicial review. The Supreme Court reversed, although without a majority opinion.

Two issues were before the Court. First: Does the federal government have the authority to hold an American citizen apprehended in a foreign country as an enemy combatant? In a 5-4 ruling, the Court said it did. Justice Sandra Day O'Connor wrote the plurality opinion, joined by Chief Justice William Rehnquist and Justices Anthony Kennedy and Stephen Breyer.

Hamdi argued that his detention violated the Non-Detention Act, which states that "no citizen shall be imprisoned or otherwise detained by the United States except pursuant to an act of Congress." The Non-Detention Act was adopted in 1971 to repeal the Emergency Detention Act of 1950, which had allowed the government, during times of emergency, to detain individuals it deemed likely to commit espionage or sabotage. As O'Connor explained, "Congress was particularly concerned about the possibility that the [Emergency Detention] Act could be used to reprise the Japanese internment camps of World War II."

But the plurality concluded that Hamdi's detention was authorized under another act of Congress: "the Authorization for Use of Military Force Joint Resolution that was passed after the September 11, 2001, terrorist attacks." O'Connor stated that the resolution provides sufficient congressional authorization to meet the requirements of the Non-Detention Act and therefore permits Hamdi's detention. Justice Clarence Thomas, in a separate opinion, concluded that the president has inherent authority, under Article II of the Constitution, to hold Hamdi as an enemy combatant.

The other four justices disagreed vehemently. In a powerful dissenting opinion, Justice Antonin Scalia, joined by Justice John Paul Stevens, argued that there is no authority to hold an American citizen in the United States as an enemy combatant without charges or a trial, unless Congress expressly suspends the writ of habeas corpus. Justice David Souter, in an opinion joined by Justice Ruth Bader Ginsburg, contended that to hold an American citizen as an enemy combatant violates the Non-Detention Act.

With five justices having ruled that the government can hold Hamdi as an enemy combatant, the Court addressed the second question: Is he entitled to due process? The Court ruled 8-1, with Thomas dissenting, that he is. Noting that imprisonment is obviously the most basic deprivation of liberty, the majority held that the government must afford due process to an American citizen apprehended in a foreign country and held as an enemy combatant.

The Right to a Meaningful Factual Hearing

The procedures required to afford due process are to be determined by applying a three-part balancing test set out in *Mathews v. Eldridge:* Courts must weigh the importance of the individual's interests, the ability of additional procedures to reduce the risk of erroneous deprivation of liberty, and the government's interests.

Although the eight justices in the majority did not specify which procedures must be followed in Hamdi's case, they held explicitly that he must be given a meaningful factual hearing. At a minimum, this includes notice of the charges, the right to respond, and the right to be represented by an attorney. However, the Court also suggested that hearsay evidence might be admissible and that the burden of proof could be placed on Hamdi.

In one sense, the Bush administration prevailed in *Hamdi:* The Court accepted its claim that it could hold U.S. citizens apprehended in a foreign country as enemy combatants. But in a more important way, the case is a significant victory for civil liberties because the Court held that even a citizen arrested on a foreign battlefield must be given a meaningful factual hearing before being detained in the United States. . . .

These rulings certainly do not resolve all the crucial issues concerning civil liberties and the war on terrorism. The administration still has not disclosed how many people have been detained. Critics believe serious abuses of rights, including unprecedented secret trials and invasions of privacy, are still occurring under the PATRIOT Act.

But with these three decisions, the Constitution—and all Americans—won. If the government position had prevailed, tomorrow you or I could be arrested and held indefinitely with no legal recourse. The Bush administration's assertion of authority to detain people without judicial review is inconsistent with the most basic constitutional principles, and the Supreme Court was right to reject it.

"Now the Supreme Court has relinquished its responsibility to protect individual liberties."

The *Hamdi* Decision Erodes Civil Liberties

Mel Lipman

Mel Lipman argues in the following viewpoint that although numerous sources have called the Hamdi v. Rumsfeld *decision a triumph for civil liberties, it is actually a serious blow to citizens' rights. For one thing, he points out,* Hamdi *upheld the detention of citizens without giving them a trial that addresses the merits of their cases. Equally concerning, Lipman writes, is that enemy combatants can be considered guilty until proven innocent, and evidence against them must meet only low standards. While the defendants are permitted to challenge their internment, Lipman adds, they still may be denied access to a lawyer and may be held for an undetermined amount of time before being given their trial. Lipman is president of the American Humanist Association, a group which promotes humanism, the philosophy that people should lead ethical lives for the greater good of humanity.*

The Supreme Court's recent [June 28, 2004] decision in the *Hamdi v. Rumsfeld* case regarding the detention of an American citizen as an "enemy combatant," along with its sister cases, is being hailed positively as the most significant civil liberties opinion in a half century. While the importance is undeniable, many organizations and news outlets mischaracterize the *Hamdi* ruling as a landmark decision in defense of the Bill of Rights. It is not.

Mel Lipman, "Guilty Until Proven Innocent: What's Missing in the Analysis of the *Hamdi* Ruling," *Humanist,* vol. 42, September 2004, pp. 42–43. Copyright © 2004 by the *Humanist.* Reproduced by permission.

After reading so many headlines declaring victory for civil liberties and defeat for the Bush administration, one can't help wondering if anyone actually read the opinions. One simple demonstration of the lack of critical reporting on this case is that nearly every news source from National Public Radio to the *Washington Times* reported the vote on the ruling as 8-1 when in fact it was 6-3, as even a casual reading of the opinions confirms.

Better Off Without *Hamdi*

Key elements of the *Hamdi* decision are glaringly absent from favorable reviews. First, the Court ruled that lower courts which hear detainee cases must shift the focal point away from the merits of the case and limit the right to fair trial by focusing only on whether the person was correctly labeled an enemy combatant. Second, the trial the Court demands turns the U.S. legal system on its head by forcing the accused to prove his or her innocence. Third, the trial described in the ruling is stripped of its usual protections against hearsay, giving nearly all the cards to the executive branch attorneys.

In reworking an important part of the U.S. government's system of checks and balances, the power of the executive branch has been inappropriately expanded. Because of this our civil liberties would be better served if there had been no decision. This opinion is a step backward that will excuse long-term imprisonments for U.S. citizens with no right to a fair trial addressing the merits of their cases.

Yes, it could have been worse. To the Court's credit the majority rightly recognized and ruled that the right to *habeas corpus*, absent suspension of that right by Congress, cannot be denied and that persons labeled as "enemy combatants" have the right to challenge, in front of a neutral decision maker, the government's evidence used to declare them as such.

Unfortunately, in the limited nature of this ruling, the majority justices overlooked the severity of the harm done when potentially innocent citizens can be imprisoned until the "end of hostilities," (perhaps indefinitely, considering the nature of the so-called war on terror) without a trial that truly addresses the merits of their alleged crimes.

A Dangerous Decision

Missing from public analysis of the decision is the way in which the Court established a new standard of "guilty until proven innocent." In an attempt to balance the competing interests of the individual and the government, the Court decided that the burden of proof would be on the defendant, who would have to show that the government's evidence was wrong or insufficient to declare him or her an enemy combatant. The Court also ruled that the government is granted to lower standards for evidence, specifically allowing it to introduce hearsay with the presumption of truth. It is hard to imagine a more egregious departure from the long-celebrated legal cornerstone of "innocent until proven guilty."

The Court fails to clarify its position on the potential for long-term, even lifelong, detention. Indeed, in her opinion, Justice Sandra Day O'Connor acknowledges that given the broad nature of the "war on terror" it could become very difficult to determine when the conflict has ended, resulting in a prolonged detention once a person is recognized as an enemy combatant.

But even the pseudo trial that the Court demands need not be held until a significant internment had already taken place. O'Connor neglects to remedy this problem and in fact leaves the door open for prolonged detainment by stating that the trial over whether or not the government is correct in its assertion that the accused is an "enemy combatant" is "only due when the determination is made to *continue to* hold those who have been seized" (emphasis added). It is dangerously unclear when the "continue to" threshold would be crossed.

Further, there is no indication in the opinion that existing domestic and international law regarding detentions will be followed. For one example, Congress' own USA PATRIOT Act allows detentions of aliens for no longer than seven days. In his dissent, Justice David Souter lends credence to this concern when he writes, "There is reason to question whether the United States is acting in accordance with the laws of war it claims to follow."

For another example, the Supreme Court ruling states that these detained "enemy combatants" may challenge their internment, but Ali Seleh Marri, a Qatar native who has been held for over a year at the Charleston Naval Consolidated Brig on charges of credit card and bank fraud, hasn't been allowed to see his attorney. Marri, who had originally been scheduled to go to trial last year [2003], until his prosecutors dropped the charges, was then designated an enemy combatant by the government. Marri's attorneys, citing the Supreme Court decision, asked in early July Assistant Solicitor General David Salmons to see their client and were then told that, according to the motion, the government would still not allow Marri to see a lawyer.

Abdicating Responsibilities

Overall, with this ruling the Court has damaged the constitutional right to a fair and speedy trial by creating separate standards, both for what the right to due process means and for what the trial must entail. Considering the nature of this decision, it is clear that when O'Connor writes, "We affirm today the fundamental nature of a citizen's right to be free from involuntary confinement," she overstates the Court's far more limited achievement.

While we're still hearing praise about this case from liberal quarters, the real story is that the *Hamdi* ruling has increased the power of the Executive, giving Bush just shy of everything he wanted. Since [the] September 11, 2001 [terrorist attacks], we seem to be witnessing the sad crumbling of the U.S. system of checks and balances. First Congress abdicated responsibility by giving the president carte blanche to make war whenever and wherever he wishes and now the Supreme Court has relinquished its responsibility to protect individual liberties. Clearly, Monday, June 28 was a somber day for civil liberties, and one made even more dour by the fact that so few even noticed the setback.

The state of civil liberties in the United States is only worse as a result of this ruling. Before the decision, public concern was rising to a high point about the way the administration was improperly detaining U.S. citizens indefinitely. Now concern is lessened as the executive branch continues to do the same thing, pausing only to undertake the formalities of a trial rigged against the detainee.

| "There's a pandemic of civil libertarian
hysteria underway."

The Rights of Suspected Terrorists Are Not Being Abused

David Tell

Critics of the War on Terror contend that terror suspects, such as Yaser Hamdi, who are detained in military custody should be granted their right to a trial. Weekly Standard *opinion editor David Tell disagrees. In the following article he insists that the civil liberties of such detainees have not been compromised. Moreover, he maintains, trying accused enemy combatants and terrorists in criminal courts is inappropriate because such suspects are unstable and are apt to incriminate themselves. Refuting assertions that the government seeks unilateral absolute power, Tell claims that the government has explained how Hamdi came to be labeled as an enemy combatant and is willing to reclassify him as a regular suspect if necessary.*

Once there was a time, while America was at war, when our government refused to grant its captured enemies, very much including the oddball U.S. citizens among them, access to the regular criminal courts. And the nation's leading newspapers and other such purveyors of advanced opinion rose up as one in reaction—and cheered. Then the Supreme Court announced it would review the situation. And the newspapers turned grumpy. Then the Supreme Court reversed course, lickety-split, and said the government's detentions and planned secret trials were a-okay. And everybody cheered again. "The niceties of jurisprudence," snorted the *Nation* (yes, the same magazine, and no, we're not making this up), "can be carried too far, and in this case the procedure was beginning to take on such overtones of fantasy that the Supreme Court's refusal to give the defendants standing in the civil courts came in the nick of time." Within days, all eight of the prisoners at issue had been tried and convicted, and six of them had been executed. News of which executions became public only after the fact. This, too, the *New York Times* approved.

Civil Libertarian Hysteria

Nowadays, in retrospect of course, President [Franklin] Roosevelt's handling of the 1942 "Nazi saboteurs" case appears rather outlandish, creepy even. No modern president would so much as dream of treating wartime detainees that way. President [George W.] Bush certainly wouldn't. "Compared to past wars led by Lincoln, Wilson, and Roosevelt, the Bush administration has diminished relatively few civil liberties," suggest the University of Chicago's Jack Goldsmith and Cass Sunstein in a forthcoming analysis of the homefront "legal culture." And yet, they note, at least "within elite circles," Bush's relatively mild prisoner-of-war policies have been met with outright horror, where Roosevelt's positively authoritarian ones were enthusiastically embraced. Why is that, they ask? The commonplace answer that Bush's detention policies stand on a weaker legal foundation than Roosevelt's, Goldsmith and Sunstein conclude, is "unpersuasive."

Instead, they argue, current editorial page denunciations of the Ashcroft Justice Department should properly be viewed as the product of a historical "ratchet effect" whereby "essential" civil liberties are conceived more expansively with every succeeding war—each conflict's specific legal "abuses," recognized as such only after armistice, being transformed into a new set of categorical taboos for the future. Goldsmith and Sunstein are nervous about this phenomenon. "The danger," they write, "is that in an age of anthrax, nuclear suitcases, and other easy-to-conceal weapons of mass destruction, the threat posed by al Qaeda and other terrorists might warrant tradeoffs between liberty and security that are inconsistent with ordinary respect for civil liberties." Ordinary respect for an ever growing list of civil liberties, that is to say, might "lead some to underestimate the threat we actually face."

One need not fully share this worry—about the practical effect of "ordinary" judicial procedures on America's capacity to defend itself against terrorism—to concur in Goldsmith and Sunstein's implied judgment that there's a pandemic of civil libertarian hysteria underway in certain "elite circles" just now. Fresh outbreaks occur on an almost daily basis. [In July 2002,] for example, at a Coronado, California, judicial conference hosted by the Ninth U.S. Circuit Court of Appeals, former Secretary of State Warren Christopher told his distinguished audience—and got a nice round of applause for it, too—that Justice Department detention policies now remind him of how, "when I was in the Carter administration, I was in Argentina and I saw mothers in the streets protesting, asking for the names of those being held, those who had disappeared." Christopher offered this spectacularly out-of-proportion analogy in direct response to a presentation by his co-panelist at the conference, Assistant Attorney General Viet Dinh. That would be the same Viet Dinh whose own father really did "disappear" into a Vietnamese reeducation camp in June 1975. Very much the way Christopher's Argentinians "disappeared." But very much *not* the way anyone has been dealt with lately here in the United States.

Now, Warren Christopher, we freely concede, is a desiccated old prune. And he plainly hasn't spent a nanosecond familiarizing himself with the particular legal questions at issue here. And what he says is fatuous. He is easy to dismiss, in other words. But it remains the case, just the same, that what

Christopher is saying, drained of its exaggeration, is what plenty of people *not* so easy to dismiss are saying, too. Therein lies a mystery.

The *Lindh* and *Hamdi* Cases

Take Stuart Taylor Jr., for instance, who, week in and week out, writes as thoughtfully and well about the law, for a non-specialist audience, as anyone in America. Here Taylor is, though, in his column for the . . . *National Journal,* raising his own version of the standard alarm about "dangers" inherent in the Bush administration's "preference for military detention over criminal prosecution" where alleged terrorists are concerned. The denouement of the John Walker Lindh trial, Taylor argues, clearly establishes that such a preference is misguided: Lindh was prosecuted in a regular, open court (more or less), where "weaknesses" in the prosecution's case could be and were exposed, and where things consequently worked out just about right. Standard procedural protocols were observed. Lindh was spared the death penalty. The government secured his assistance in its ongoing investigations. Neat.

Where the Justice Department has skirted the courts and incarcerated al Qaeda suspects as "enemy combatants" by "fiat," however, Taylor would have it that nothing is neat— indeed that everything we most cherish about our legal system is in peril. Look, he says, at Yasser Hamdi, the U.S. citizen taken prisoner with his Taliban unit in Afghanistan, who is now being held—without criminal charge—in a Norfolk, Virginia, Navy brig. The "enemy combatant" designation being used to justify Hamdi's detention is completely unreviewable by the federal courts, according to the government, according to Stuart Taylor. Hamdi almost certainly *is* an "enemy combatant," granted. But what about others like him who might similarly fall into the Defense Department's clutches? Are they to be hidden away forever, denied any chance to establish their innocence to an independent authority, in a radical "departure ... from centuries of Anglo-American jurisprudence"?

The Truth About Terror Suspects in Federal Courts

We find it difficult to account for such complaints merely by reference to real-world facts. About the *Lindh* case, we would point out that its defendant, the suburban California teenager cum Wahhabi lunatic, was hardly the kind of fellow our Marines are likely to confront very often on the battlefield. Moreover, Lindh's sentence, rather than signaling "weaknesses" in the indictment lodged against him, looks more to us like the typical leniency-for-cooperation plea bargain of a guy who sort of wishes he could be a suburban California teenager once again. The *Lindh* case, in short, may not be the best crystal ball through which to predict what regular criminal prosecutions of al Qaeda operatives would entail.

Zacarias Moussaoui, whom Stuart Taylor neglects to mention, is the more obvious—and disturbing—model. Moussaoui is now being given every inch of the civil-court trial the Justice Department's critics think generally appropriate. And the early results—even, or perhaps especially, from a civil libertarian perspective—do not look good. A man would have to have a heart of stone to read the transcript of Moussaoui's rearraignment hearing [in July 2002] without quailing a little. Unlike Lindh, apparently, Moussaoui really means it: He hates and mistrusts America. And so he hates and mistrusts America's courts. And so he is representing himself *pro se*— and in the process he is committing slow-motion suicide, without even realizing it, while a talented and conscientious U.S. district judge, Leonie Brinkema, vainly tries to protect his interests.

> **Moussaoui:** I will be able to prove that I have certain knowledge of September 11, and I know exactly who done it. I know which group, who participated, when it was decided. I have many information. ... I, Moussaoui Zacarias, in the

interests to preserve my life, enter with full conscience a plea of guilty, because I have knowledge and participated in, in al Qaeda. I am a member of al Qaeda.

Brinkema: Mr. Moussaoui, you have to stop, or I'll have the marshals remove you.

Moussaoui: I pledge *bayat* [allegiance] to [al Qaeda leader] Osama bin Laden. . . . I am guilty.

At this rate, precisely *because* he has been accorded full access to the regular federal courts, Zacarias Moussaoui, the gears of those courts grinding away in their regular fashion, is going to win himself a lethal injection—even though the case against him remains entirely circumstantial. Does the fact that it all will be "his fault" make it any less an embarrassment?

Suspects' Rights Are Protected

And mightn't Yasser Hamdi and the other "enemy combatants" being held in military custody thus be better off where they are? After all, as we read the Justice Department's filings in Hamdi's ongoing *habeas corpus* proceedings, it simply isn't true—as nearly every editorial page would have it—that our government is claiming unilateral, absolute power to call people "enemy combatants" and lock them up for the rest of time. In fact, in the *Hamdi* case itself, the government has already offered for judicial review a sealed submission that Chief Judge Harvie Wilkinson of the Fourth Circuit says "specifically delineates the manner in which the military assesses and screens enemy combatants to determine who among them should be brought under Department of Defense control" and further "describes how the military determined that petitioner Hamdi fit the eligibility requirements applied to enemy combatants for detention." What's more, Justice Department lawyers have themselves acknowledged, by reference to Supreme

Court precedents which suggest as much explicitly, that the judiciary may "call upon the executive to provide 'some evidence' supporting [enemy combatant] determination[s]"—and may also, by logical extension, invalidate such determinations if it turns out the evidence is wholly insubstantial.

How on earth does any of this constitute an outrage against American civil liberties, much less a "departure . . . from centuries of Anglo-American jurisprudence"? And why—given that the executive branch, dispassionately observed, has neither proposed nor claimed authority nor otherwise shown the slightest willingness to pursue the war on terrorism with wild, extra-legal abandon—are so many smart people among us nevertheless disposed to regard the U.S. government as a dangerous, snarling beast?

"The Supreme Court did not take on, and in fact endorsed, the president's enormous grab for . . . power."

The President Has Too Much Power over Terror Suspects

C. Clark Kissinger

During the War on Terror, President George W. Bush ordered the military to hold some terror suspects (including American citizens) until the end of hostilities without affording them due process. The Supreme Court ruled in Hamdi v. Rumsfeld *that in such cases the minimum requirements of due process must be met, but the usual standards can be lowered. In the viewpoint that follows, political activist C. Clark Kissinger accuses the Court of bowing to Bush's demands for power. In deciding that the president may authorize the detention of suspects without a hearing, the Court allowed him to continue essentially kidnapping citizens of America and other countries in violation of domestic and international law, Kissinger asserts. In addition, he notes, the Court mentioned that in enemy combatant hearings, military tribunals could serve as neutral decision makers. Kissinger suggests such tribunals cannot be neutral. The Court's rulings, in his opinion, allow the government to move toward fascist rule.*

On June 28 [2004] the U.S. Supreme Court decided on three major cases that challenged the President's use of the military to kidnap people, label them "enemy combatants," and imprison them indefinitely solely on his say-so—without charges, access to an attorney, and judicial review. The cases stemmed from petitions brought against the holding of hun-

C. Clark Kissinger, "The Meaning of the Supreme Court's Decision on 'Enemy Combatants,'" *Revolutionary Worker,* July 18, 2004, p. 3.

dreds of foreign nationals at the U.S. naval base at Guantánamo, Cuba, and the holding of two U.S. citizens—Jose Padilla and Yaser Hamdi—at a naval base in Charleston, S.C.

The Court's decisions were widely described in the media as a big setback for [George W.] Bush. A statement from Justice Sandra Day O'Connor has been widely quoted—that "a state of war is not a blank check for the President when it comes to the rights of the Nation's citizens."

But little quoted in the media were O'Connor's other assertions—that "there is no bar to this Nation's holding one of its own citizens as an enemy combatant" and that rather than "innocent until proven guilty," the burden is on the imprisoned citizen to prove that he or she is *not* an "enemy combatant."

Writing in the *Wall Street Journal,* John Yoo, until recently an Assistant Attorney General in the Bush administration, made a revealing comment: "The justices implicitly recognized that the U.S. may use all the tools of war to fight a new kind of enemy.... Taken as a whole, the Court's message is unmistakable: The days when terrorism was merely considered a law enforcement problem and our only forces were limited to the FBI, federal prosecutors and the criminal justice system will not be returning."

Legal Kidnappings

While the Supreme Court did not give the President a blank check, it did give him a Gold Card with a very generous credit limit. The Supreme Court is not some neutral arbiter of justice. It is an integral part of the capitalist state that usually plays a more "stepped back" role in relation to the immediate policies of any administration and looks to the longer-term interests of the ruling class as a whole. (Of course, in the disputed Florida elections in 2000, the Supreme Court played a direct role in getting Bush & Co. into the White House.)

So the high court was trying to deal with certain contradictions for the ruling class arising from what Bush, [Vice President Dick] Cheney, and [Secretary of Defense Donald] Rumsfeld are hell-bent on doing around the world. There is a continuing contradiction with U.S. allies over holding their citizens in violation of international law at Guantánamo. British Prime Minister Tony Blair has been greatly weakened for allowing the U.S. to kidnap British citizens and hold them at Guantánamo with no legal rights.

There is also the tremendous fallout from the prison torture scandal at Abu Ghraib [Iraq]. This put pressure on the Supreme Court to at least take some cosmetic steps—especially after the following dialogue that took place in the oral arguments before the Court on May 27 [2004], just days before the torture scandal broke:

Justice [Ruth] Ginsburg: "But if the law is what the executive says it is, whatever is necessary and appropriate in the executive's judgment . . . what is it that would be a check against torture?"

Answer by the government: "Well, first of all there are treaty obligations."

Even as the government lawyer was talking about international treaties, this very same administration was shuffling around memos that sought to manufacture arguments for ignoring international treaties and laws in order to justify the torture of prisoners.

Case Background

The case of Jose Padilla was perhaps the strongest challenge to the newly asserted presidential powers to arrest citizens and hold them without charges. Padilla was arrested in the U.S. by the FBI and turned over to the military only after he contested his detention in court. The Supreme Court dodged the issue entirely, dismissing his petition on the grounds that it should have been filed in South Carolina where he is held now, rather than in New York where he was originally held. Padilla, who has now been held for over two years, will continue to be imprisoned under the same outrageous conditions and must start all over with a new court-appointed lawyer in South Carolina. (For the background on these cases, see "Dangerous Presidential Powers: From Citizen to 'Enemy Combatant,'" *RW* [*Revolutionary Worker*] #1236, April 11, 2004, and online at rwor.org.)

Yaser Hamdi was captured by the Northern warlords in the Aghanistan civil war and turned over to the U.S. In the *Hamdi* case, the Supreme Court did set some parameters for how "enemy combatants" will now be handled. The Court held that Hamdi could have access to a lawyer and that he must have an opportunity to contest his designation as an "enemy combatant" before some "neutral decisionmaker." The court split four ways with four different opinions. A look at these four opinions gives a view of the spectrum of ruling class opinion on these issues.

Four Opinions

First, Clarence Thomas supported the Bush administration 100%, saying that the courts had no business second-guessing the president's use of the military to fight "terrorists." Second, Antonin Scalia (joined by Justice [John] Stevens) said that unless the Congress officially suspends the right of habeas corpus, the president has no right to imprison U.S. citizens as "enemy combatants." If there is evidence that someone was fighting with an enemy against the U.S., they should be prosecuted for treason.

Third, four justices (O'Connor, [William] Rehnquist, [Anthony] Kennedy and [Stephen] Breyer) said that these first two views are wrong. They said there must be some mechanism for prisoners to contest their designation as "enemy combatants." At the same time, that cannot be a full-blown court trial. And they said the president does have the power to detain people without trial. The justification they put forward is that such detention is to prevent the alleged "enemy combatants" from rejoining the enemy forces. It is not a punishment, and therefore the detainees are not entitled to rights given a criminal defendant!

Fourth, Justice [David] Souter (joined by Justice Ginsburg) wrote that the Non Detention Act of 1971 required that no one could be detained as an "enemy combatant" except by the authority of a law passed by Congress. The administration has claimed the Congressional grant of authority to use military force (of September 15, 2001) implicitly gave the president this authority. Souter and Ginsburg complain that it had to be explicit to be official, but they agreed with the four justices above that in any case there had to be access to lawyers and a chance for the prisoner to contest the allegations.

The effect of these various opinions is 1) that anyone (citizen or not) detained in U.S. territory as an "enemy combatant" has a right to see a lawyer and contest their status before some "neutral decisionmaker," and 2) the president can indeed designate persons (including citizens) as "enemy combatants" and detain them for the "duration of the conflict." And the "duration of the conflict" could be generations, as the government has frequently pointed out.

The Supreme Court did not take on, and in fact endorsed, the president's enormous grab for the power, in the name of presidential "war powers," to deal with alleged enemies as he sees fit, outside the scope of either domestic or international law. This can only lead to the deployment of the military against political opponents of the state and to the designation of political opponents of U.S. wars and interventions as "enemy combatants," based on accusations that they are giving support to enemies of U.S. imperialism or anyone standing in its way.

In short, the high court has put no real brake on the government's quickening moves toward a more fascistic form of rule.

Military Tribunals Endorsed

In the case of the approximately 600 prisoners from 42 different countries held at Guantánamo, the Bush administration lawyers had made the ridiculous argument that U.S. courts had no jurisdiction at Guantánamo because it was "sovereign Cuban territory." The Supreme Court ruled that U.S. courts did have jurisdiction over what happened at Guantánamo and prisoners held there could contest their status as "enemy combatants."

At the same time, the Court was very careful to point out that this did not necessarily mean a day in court. As O'Connor wrote for the plurality of the court: "There remains the possibility that the standards we have articulated could be met by an appropriately authorized and properly constituted military tribunal. . . . In the absence of such process, however, a court that receives a petition for a writ of habeas corpus from an alleged enemy combatant must itself ensure the minimum requirements of due process are achieved." Here O'Connor was telling the administration, "If you guys don't want these cases to come into the courts, you'd better get your military tribunals up and running."

O'Connor went on to elaborate how such tribunals needn't trouble themselves with the niceties of protecting prisoners' rights: "Enemy combatant proceedings may be tailored to alleviate their uncommon potential to burden the Executive at a time of ongoing military conflict. Hearsay, for example, may need to be accepted as the most reliable available evidence from the government in such a proceeding. Likewise, the Constitution would not be offended by a presumption in favor of the government's evidence . . . the onus could shift to the petitioner to rebut that evidence with more persuasive evidence that he falls outside the criteria."

This makes a mockery of justice. How are prisoners held incommunicado for over three years—without access to lawyers, investigators, family, newspapers, mail, or telephones—supposed to be able to prove that they are NOT "enemy combatants"?

It didn't take long for the administration to pick up on this roadmap on how to set up a kangaroo court. On July 7 [2004], the Defense Department announced that it had created a new "Combatant Status Review Tribunal" consisting of three military officers. This is the "neutral decisionmaker" before which the Guantánamo prisoners can try to prove that they have been wrongly held as "enemy combatants." The military claims that these officers would be neutral because they have no personal interest in the status of particular detainees. (Apparently their personal interest in getting their next promotion from the Commander-in-Chief is not a problem.)

At the same time, the Defense Department announced that more detainees at Guantánamo will be actually charged with crimes and tried before a military tribunal of five officers, which could sentence them to death.

Finally, the most scandalous aspect of the whole detainees issue has been effectively swept under the rug. The hundreds of detainees at Guantánamo and the two U.S. citizens being held by the military in the U.S. are actually the low-level "suspects." Prisoners who are considered high-level leaders of the Taliban, al-Qaida, the Iraqi resistance, or whatever have been spirited away to secret locations in countries where they can be tortured with no prospect of interference or exposure. "The Disappeared," an ABC *Nightline* program of May 13 [2004], reported that all this has been done under secret orders to the CIA signed by President Bush in early 2002.

Organizations to Contact

American Bar Association (ABA)
740 Fifteenth St. NW
Washington, DC 20005
(202) 662-1000
e-mail: service@abanet.org • Web site: www.abanet.org

As the world's largest voluntary professional association, the ABA represents the legal profession on a national level and serves to promote justice and respect for the law. To this end, the ABA provides law school accreditation, programs to assist judges and lawyers, and initiatives to improve the legal system. Its publications include the monthly *ABA Journal* and the quarterly magazine *Criminal Justice.*

American Civil Liberties Union (ACLU)
125 Broad St., Eighteenth Floor
New York, NY 10004
(212) 549-2500
e-mail: aclu@aclu.org • Web site: www.aclu.org

The ACLU is a national organization that works to defend Americans' civil rights guaranteed by the U.S. Constitution. It opposes random searches, speech codes, and certain provisions of the Patriot Act. The ACLU offers policy statements, pamphlets, the semiannual newsletter *Civil Liberties Alert,* and press releases with titles such as "In Defense of Freedom in a Time of Crisis."

The Brookings Institution
1775 Massachusetts Ave. NW
Washington, DC 20036
(202) 797-6000 • fax: (202) 797-6004
e-mail: brookinfo@brook.edu • Web site: www.brookings.org

The institution, founded in 1927, is a think tank that conducts research and education in foreign policy, economics, government, and the social sciences. In 2001 it began America's Response to Terrorism, a project that provides briefings and analysis to the public and which is featured on the center's Web site. Other publications include the quarterly *Brookings Review*, periodic *Policy Briefs*, and books such as *Terrorism and U.S. Foreign Policy*.

CATO Institute
1000 Massachusetts Ave. NW
Washington, DC 20001
(202) 842-0200 • fax: (202) 842-3490
e-mail: cato@cato.org • Web site: www.cato.org

The institute is a nonpartisan public policy research foundation dedicated to limiting the role of government and protecting individual liberties. It publishes the quarterly magazine *Regulation*, the bimonthly *Cato Policy Report*, and numerous policy papers and articles. "Does U.S. Intervention Overseas Breed Terrorism?" and "Military Tribunals No Answer" are among its works on terrorism.

Center for Defense Information
1779 Massachusetts Ave. NW, Suite 615
Washington, DC 20036
(202) 332-0600 • fax: (202) 462-4559
e-mail: info@cdi.org • Web site: www.cdi.org

The Center for Defense Information is a nonpartisan, nonprofit organization that researches all aspects of global security. It seeks to educate the public and policy makers about issues such as weapons systems, security policy, and defense budgeting. It produces the monthly publication *Defense Monitor*, the issue brief "National Missile Defense: What Does It All Mean?" and studies including "Homeland Security: A Competitive Strategies Approach."

Center for Immigration Studies
1522 K St. NW, Suite 820
Washington, DC 20005-1202
(202) 466-8185 • fax: (202) 466-8076

e-mail: center@cis.org • Web site: www.cis.org

The center studies the effects of immigration on the economic, social, demographic, and environmental conditions in the United States. It believes that the large number of recent immigrants has become a burden on America and favors reforming immigration laws to make them more consistent with U.S. interests. The organization's editorials, reports, and position papers are available on its Web site, which offers a link for "Terrorism & National Security."

The Heritage Foundation
214 Massachusetts Ave. NE
 Washington, DC   20002-4999
(800) 544-4843 • fax: (202) 544-2260
e-mail: pubs@heritage.org • Web site: www.heritage.org

The foundation is a conservative public policy organization dedicated to free-market principles, individual liberty, and limited government. It favors limiting freedom of the press when that freedom threatens national security. Its resident scholars publish position papers on a wide range of issues through publications such as the weekly *Backgrounder* and the quarterly *Policy Review.*

National Coalition Against Censorship (NCAC)
275 Seventh Ave., New York, NY 10001
(212) 807-6222 • fax: (212) 807-6245
e-mail: ncac@ncac.org • Web site: www.ncac.org

NCAC is an alliance of organizations committed to defending freedom of thought, inquiry, and expression by engaging in public education and advocacy on national and local levels. NCAC prints periodic reports and the quarterly *Censorship News.* Its Web site section, NCAC on the Issues, contains a link for "Government Secrecy & Censorship in Wartime."

National Security Agency
9800 Savage Rd., Ft. Meade, MD   20755-6248

(301) 688-6524
Web site: www.nsa.gov

The National Security Agency coordinates, directs, and performs activities which protect American information systems and produce foreign intelligence information. It is also one of the most important centers of foreign language analysis and research within the government. Speeches, briefings, and reports are available on the Web site.

People for the American Way (PFAW)
2000 M St. NW, Suite 400
 Washington, DC 20036
(202) 467-4999
e-mail: pfaw@pfaw.org • Web site: www.pfaw.org

PFAW is committed to reaffirming the traditional American values of pluralism, diversity, and freedom of expression and religion in many areas, including education. It is engaged in a mass media campaign to create a climate of tolerance and respect for diverse people, religions, and values. PFAW distributes educational materials, leaflets, brochures, and annual publications.

For Further Research

Books

George W. Bush, Peggy Noonan, and Jay Nordlinger, *We Will Prevail: President George W. Bush on War, Terrorism, and Freedom.* New York: Continuum, 2003.

Elaine Cassel, *The War on Civil Liberties: How Bush and Ashcroft Have Dismantled the Bill of Rights.* New York: Lawrence Hill Books, 2004.

Zechariah Chafee, *Freedom of Speech.* New York: Harcourt, Brace, and Howe, 1920.

David Cole and James X. Dempsey, *Terrorism and the Constitution: Sacrificing Civil Liberties in the Name of National Security.* Tallahassee, FL: First Amendment Foundation, 2002.

Nancy C. Cornwell, *Freedom of the Press: Rights and Liberties Under the Law.* Santa Barbara, CA: ABC-CLIO, 2004.

M. Katherine B. Darmer, Robert M. Baird, and Stuart E. Rosenbaum, eds., *Civil Liberties vs. National Security in a Post 9/11 World.* Amherst, NY: Prometheus, 2004.

Alan Dershowitz, *Shouting Fire: Civil Liberties in a Turbulent Age.* New York: Little, Brown, 2002.

Owen M. Fiss, *The Irony of Free Speech.* Cambridge, MA: Harvard University Press, 1998.

Charles Fried, *Saying What the Law Is.* Cambridge, MA: Harvard University Press, 2004.

Martin Garbus, *Courting Disaster: The Supreme Court and the Unmaking of American Law.* New York: Times Books, Henry Holt, 2002.

Morton Grodzing, *Americans Betrayed: Politics and the Japanese Evacuations.* Chicago: University of Chicago Press, 1949.

Thomas R. Hensley, ed., *The Boundaries of Freedom of Expression and Order in American Democracy.* Kent, OH: Kent State University Press, 2001.

Karl F. Inderfurth and Loch K. Johnson, eds., *Fateful Decisions: Inside the National Security Council.* Oxford, UK: Oxford University Press, 2004.

Ronald Kessler, *The CIA at War: Inside the Secret Campaign Against Terror.* New York: Griffin, 2004.

Mark M. Lowenthal, *Intelligence: From Secrets to Policy.* Washington, DC: CQ Press, 2003.

Michelle Malkin, *In Defense of Internment: The Case for "Racial Profiling" in World War II and the War on Terror.* Washington, DC: Regnery, 2004.

Richard A. Parker, ed., *Free Speech on Trial.* Tuscaloosa: University of Alabama Press, 2003.

John Prados and Margaret Pratt Porter, *Inside the Pentagon Papers.* Lawrence: University Press of Kansas, 2004.

William H. Rehnquist, *All the Laws but One.* New York: Alfred A. Knopf, 1998.

Relocation of Japanese Americans. Washington, DC: War Relocation Authority, 1943.

Wojciech Sadurski, *Freedom of Speech and Its Limits.* New York: Kluwer, 2002.

Geoffrey R. Stone, *Perilous Times: Free Speech in Wartime from the Sedition Act of 1798 to the War on Terrorism.* New York: W.W. Norton & Co., 2004.

Sanford J. Ungar, *The Papers & The Papers.* New York: E.P. Dutton, 1972.

Samuel Walker, *Civil Liberties in America: A Reference Handbook.* Santa Barbara, CA: ABC-CLIO, 2004.

Periodicals

American Civil Liberties Union, "Freedom of Expression," January 2, 1997. www.aclu.org.

Bradford A. Berenson and Richard Klingler, "Justice Served— Nabbing Illegal Aliens Isn't a Violation of Civil Rights," *Wall Street Journal,* June 9, 2003.

Zechariah Chafee Jr., "Freedom of Speech in Time of War," *Harvard Law Review,* 1919.

S. Olney Cutler, "The Clear and Present Danger Test—*Schenck* to *Dennis,*" *Georgetown Law Journal,* January 1952.

Ted DeCorte, "The Red Scare in Nevada, 1919–1920," News Mine.org, 2002. www.newsmine.org.

Christopher Dunn, "The Supreme Court and Civil Liberties During Times of War," *New York Law Journal,* October 25, 2001.

Terry Eastland, "How Danger Becomes 'Clear and Present,'" *Weekly Standard,* October 8, 2002.

Leslie Gelb, "Lessons from the Pentagon Papers," *Life,* September 17, 1971.

Stephanie Elizondo Griest, "'Clear and Present Danger' or 'All Is Fair in Love and War,'" The Odyssey: U.S. Trek. www.us trek.org.

Norman Hapgood, "Oases of Freedom," *Nation,* February 9, 1921.

Arthur G. Hayes, "Civil Liberties in War Time," *Bill of Rights Review,* Spring 1942.

Gerard C. Henderson, "What Is Left of Free Speech," *New Republic,* December 10, 1919.

Henry Mark Holzer, "Civil Liberties Hysteria," FrontPageMaga zine.com, July 2, 2003. www.frontpagemagazine.com.

Carlos A. Kelly, "The Pen Is Mightier than the Sword or Why the Media Should Exercise Self-Restraint in Time of War," *Florida Bar Journal,* January 2003.

Edward Lazarus, "Why the U.S. Court of Appeals Opinion in the Jose Padilla Case Is Not Anti-Government but Pro-Democracy," FindLaw, January 15, 2004. www.findlaw.com.

Anthony Lewis, "A Free, Informed, and Courageous Press Insures National Security," March 2, 2004. www.cardozo. yu.edu.

Abraham Lincoln, "Letter to Erastus Corning and Others," June 12, 1863. www.teachingamericanhistory.org.

Walter Lippman, "The Fifth Column on the Coast," *Los Angeles Times*, February 12, 1942.

Adam Liptak, Neil A. Lewis, and Benjamin Weiser, "After Sept. 11, a Legal Battle on the Limits of Civil Liberty," *New York Times*, August 4, 2002.

Nelson Lund, "The Conservative Case Against Racial Profiling in the War on Terrorism," *Albany Law Review*, 2003.

Heather MacDonald, "Taking Dictation from the ACLU," *Weekly Standard*, October 18, 2004.

Nation, "Are American Liberties Worth Saving?" April 17, 1920.

New York Times, "Excerpts from Latest Editorial Reaction in U.S. and Abroad to Publication of Documents on Vietnam War," June 18, 1971.

Michelle Parrini and Charles F. Williams, "Enemy Combatants and the Courts," *Social Education*, March 2005.

John Podesta, "America's Secret History: Securing Our Future by Embracing Open Government," March 10, 2004. www.americanprogress.org.

Richard A. Posner, "The Truth About Our Liberties," *Responsive Community*, Summer 2002.

Jesselyn Radack, "How the 'Enemy Combatant' Label Is Being Used, Part 2," Findlaw, October 11, 2004. www.findlaw.com.

Anita Ramasastry, "A Flawed Report Card: How DOJ Mishandled the Post–September 11 Detention Process," Find-Law, August 1, 2003.

Jeffrey Rosen, "A Lesson in Liberties," *Washington Post*, September 23–29, 2002.

San Francisco News, "Their Best Way to Show Loyalty," March 6, 1942.

Harvey Silverglate, "Civil Liberties and Enemy Combatants," *Reason*, January 2005.

Hedrick Smith, "Mitchell Seeks to Halt Series on Vietnam, but *Times* Refuses," *New York Times*, June 15, 1971.

Bruce J. Terris, "Common Sense in Profiling," *Midstream,* February/March 2002.

Mark V. Tushnet, "Defending Korematsu?: Reflections on Civil Liberties in Wartime," *Wisconsin Law Review,* 2003.

Michael M. Uhlmann, "The Supreme Court Rules: 2004," *First Things,* October 2004.

Web sites

Findlaw (www.findlaw.com). This site contains extensive archives of Supreme Court and lower court decisions, a helpful search engine, and links to other important legal information. Analyses of court decisions are also provided by Findlaw's numerous commentators.

Legal Information Institute (http://supct.law.cornell.edu/supct). The Legal Information Institute archives the opinions and dissents in historical Supreme Court decisions as well as in recent rulings. The Web site also offers updates on current Supreme Court cases.

Index